Out of the Fowler's Snare

Roseanne J. Sanderfoot

Printed in the United States of America
First Printing, 2017

ISBN-13: 978-1548535025
ISBN-10: 1548535028

Disclaimer:
Some names and identifying details have been changed to
protect the privacy of individuals.

The information presented in this memoir is intended to be for
your educational and entertainment purposes only. We will
not share in your success, nor will we be responsible for your
failure or for your actions in any endeavor you may undertake
as a result of reading this book. We wish you every success in
finding wholeness, but take no responsibility for your actions
or healing.

Dedication

This book is dedicated to all of the wounded souls that have been damaged by purposeful and intentional bullying. For whatever reason, you were singled out as being different, and targeted because of those supposed differences. Like me, possibly you had no clue why someone (or many) might want to harm you. You were likely minding your own business, just trying to live your life the best you knew how, and out of nowhere came the first of many hurtful words and actions that took you by such pained surprise.

Maybe it was just one empowered bully or maybe it became many. In any case, you felt weakened, defenseless and voiceless. While others likely saw the onslaught, no one stepped in to suitably rescue you. The pain of what you experienced became a part of who you would turn out to be. In all likelihood, that injury will permanently be part of that total being called YOU. Your strengths, weaknesses, hopes, dreams, and human relationships are now entwined with what you experienced alone. Although the hurt of victimization can last for decades, I want you to know that there is hope and help, and it may come in a most unexpected way, as it did for me. The pain that seems to be unending doesn't have to last a lifetime. There is freedom from it, and one day, I trust and pray that you will find that you, too, have been released from the fowler's snare. May you escape like a bird to find your freedom! Your help is in the name of the Lord, the One who made you to fly!

"I don't think books take off and do well,
or don't do well, depending just on the quality of
the writing. I think it depends on catching something
that's in the air, something that people need."

John Sherrill, Writer for Guideposts

(From *David Wilkerson: The Cross, the
Switchblade, and the Man Who Believed)*

Foreword

I began reading this book, at first glance, out of
duty. Then I could not put it down. Quickly I was
absorbed and immersed. Roseanne has a flair for
honest and vivid writing. This very real, sometimes
painful, often powerful, personal account of bullying
exposes a scarred life, yet a cheeringly brave one. I've
known Roseanne, in the time that we worked together
as therapist/client, to be both timid and tenacious, a
powerful combination! Since that time she has grown
in ways that inspire me and will challenge the reader.
Readers will be encouraged to be aware and
charitable as they tune in to both the inner life of a
harassed teen and a powerful grown-up. The reader
will also have a window to the inmost being of
someone seeking ways to heal, sometimes in helpful
ways, sometimes damaging. Roseanne is a humble
and strong heroine. She does not pull punches.
Honesty is one of the many gifts you will find in this
memoir. The book is a pattern of walking through
personal devastation to a healthy understanding of
love. You will be enriched by this true story of pain
and ultimate success. This is a book in which many

teens and adults will find hope and a map of one way through the effects of bullying and victimization.

Lynda Savage, MS, LMFT, LPC
Founder/Therapist: Center for Family Healing (Menasha, WI)
Founder/Radio Host: Practical Family Living

Author's Preface

This book has been in the making for about 40 years. But, only for the last two decades have I felt that it was my actual destiny to write a book about the story that became so much a part of who I am. At various times in conversation, when I would skirt the issue of writing a book without ever saying much about the topic, friends and acquaintances would always give me encouragement to do so. When they would see me, they would occasionally ask if I had started the book yet. The answer was always, "No, but, it's in my head. I have the title."

Finally in the spring of 2006, I decided that it was time to get started. I was just waiting until June when my teaching year was complete, and then I was going to get going. About the time my school year ended in June, my husband was permanently laid off from his telecom job. He was home and underfoot, and I could see that the summer of 2006 was not going to work for writing a book. I again put the idea on hold and told my encouragers that I really didn't have a clue how the book was going to end anyway.

As the school year was nearing an end in 2008 I thought that this was the year that I would start my book. I decided that beginning on the first day of my summer vacation, I was going to commit to writing 4 days each week, for 2 hours each day. My plan was to get up early each day, take the dog out for a walk, take time for prayer and a Bible devotional, and then get to work. I did not want the book to consume my life and I was worried about the emotional toll that it might take on me.

Right on schedule and according to plan, I sat down to write. I was thrilled because things seemed to be going so well. I was feeling good about how the words seemed to flow easily onto the page. I was on a bit of a "high" after the first week of writing. I even told a few more people about my venture.

Unfortunately, on the sixth day of writing, I went to open my files and found—nothing. All of my files were gone! I was absolutely sick! I waited to call my husband until his workday was almost done. I didn't want to trash his day just because my dream and my destiny were shot to heck. When he came home from work, he spent his entire evening trying to retrieve and reestablish my book. He felt that the files were gone for good. Knowing that he was a troubleshooter and much more computer savvy than me, I knew he was probably right.

At that point, I needed a padded room to kick, scream, cry, and wail in privacy. I didn't have one. I was afraid that even if I went into the basement and screamed into a pillow with all the windows in the house closed, the neighbors would probably still hear me and wonder what terrible crime was being committed. I was simply crushed, and believed that my dream of writing a book was gone, thanks to computer technology. How could my life's destiny be dashed on the rocks so easily?

Hubby Mike was not much help, offering his thought that it was "only a minor setback." Coming from a man who struggles to write a greeting card, it seemed to ring hollow for me. But, technologically, he did do all that he could and asked the computer geeks that he knew for advice. They all agreed that the book was probably gone for good. Spiritually, he prayed that God would help me find a way to deal with my loss.

It took about a week for me to accept the fact that for whatever reasons the book was, indeed, gone. I didn't know why God allowed it to happen, but what could I do to change it? Maybe He was protecting me from hurt by deleting the book before it got too far. Maybe it really wasn't my destiny, and I had believed wrongly for 20 years. It felt like I was without hope, without a future, and without a dream.

I told God that if He wanted the book written, if it was His will, then He would have to restore the files. I felt that I did not have it in me to start over, at least not this year. And besides, if it was not His will, why would I want to start it over anyway? I needed to let go of the book. If God wanted it done, He was certainly capable of restoring the computer files. Otherwise, I was done with the dream. I even crossed out "dreams" on my daily prayer list.

Since I had told a few more people about my starting a book that summer, it was inevitable that people would ask how the writing was going. It was embarrassing, but I had to admit what had happened. I was just so happy that I hadn't told more people than the few that I did tell. Those who heard of the lost files agreed with Mike that it probably was just a small setback. Not in my mind. I didn't feel that I had it in my heart to start over. It was in God's hands, and I boldly stated that if God wanted it done, He could restore the files and that was that. Over the course of the next month, everyone who knew of the book had been told what had happened. I no longer had to avoid anyone to avoid talking about it. I still felt sad about the loss of a dream, but I accepted my reality.

One evening in late July, Mike had been printing some things off the Internet for our planned vacation while I cleaned up the dinner dishes. He quietly came out to the kitchen and said, "I think I have your book back. Come and see if it's all there." I stopped breathing momentarily and advised him strongly not to mess with me. I didn't know whether to cry or shout praises to the Lord, but I was literally shaking. He had me come to our home office and check over the files to see if the writing was all there. Most of it seemed to be—but, I was hesitant to believe it. Mike told me that one of the techno-geeks at work must have been mentally working over the problem for the last three weeks and asked him if he had tried a certain procedure. Mike asked him a few further questions, of which he had no specific answers. It was a few days later when he was printing out the vacation information and decided to give the procedure a try. Because he didn't want to raise any of my hopes needlessly, he didn't say anything until he was pretty sure that the book was at least somewhat restored. Even as I saw my words back on the computer screen, I felt a certain caution to believe that God had worked a miracle and restored my book, my dream, and my destiny.

For the next three weeks, I didn't even open my book files. I was overwhelmed with the whole concept that God had brought restoration to the dream and that it must be His will for the book to go forward. It seemed a huge responsibility to write a book and know without any shadow of doubt that it was God's will for it to be written. I had to let it sink in that the book was God's will, not just my dream alone. I needed to rest in knowing that since it was His will, He would bring it to fruition in His planning and timing. What an awesome dream to fulfill...the writing of God's story in my life!

Acknowledgments

First and foremost, I am grateful to God who has released me from the snare that bound me for so very long. You have helped me find the JOY that was my namesake and destiny. You have redeemed my life, and it is Yours.

A big hug of thanks to my husband Mike, who walked through the years of struggle with me. You patiently stayed by my side and loved me well as I stumbled and limped along searching for the key to my healing. I believe you are enjoying the new me, too!

With deep appreciation, I acknowledge my large and wonderful family of origin. I'm sorry that I kept this deep ugly secret from you. It was the only thing I knew to do at the time. In hindsight, I know you would have joined forces around me, both in prayer and in the physical; you would not have left me to fend for myself.

To my parents especially, thank you for all the prayers that you prayed on my behalf! Mom, I know as "the Mother Bear", you would have done anything to protect me had you known at the time. I knew this book would never be published while you were alive because it would have brought you much grief and sadness. But, I also know that you are now in the "great cloud of witnesses" cheering me on! (Hebrews 12:1/See Appendix for full scripture.) Dad, you made it so easy to trust in a Father God because of how you lived your daily life. You were a man of integrity, patience, and strength who always modeled the importance of a positive attitude. Thank you, both, for your great faith that gives me great faith!

A sincere thank you to Lynda Savage (MS, LMTF, LPC) founder and therapist at *The Center for Family Healing, Inc.* in Menasha, WI for helping me take the first baby steps on a good path. While the "fix" didn't come as quickly as I wanted, you taught me to invite Jesus into every aspect of my life.

Thanks to Lori, Sharon, and Howard, those few compassionate high school friends who undoubtedly had a part in keeping me from suicide. Although you didn't know it, you were part of my rescue.

Thanks also to dear Ms. Sandra Wittman, my high school English teacher, who helped me believe I could write well.

With deep sincerity, I am so very grateful for the spiritual mentors in my young teenaged life. Specifically, I mention Billy and Patti Smith, my school principal and his wife, who opened their home on Sunday nights to a motley crew of youths from all faiths and none. You helped us find Jesus and start on a walk as one of His.

Although now deceased, my spiritual life was richly impacted by Pastor David R. Wilkerson, author of *The Cross and the Switchblade* (1962), who played a huge role in helping me to make my faith my own and encouraged me to be a Jesus Person of the '70s. His worldwide youth crusades have made an eternal difference for me and others.

With love, laughter, and abundant joy, I thank my dearest friends who always treated me as valuable even when they didn't understand the wounded places in my soul. You loved and accepted me and made me feel cherished, as only true friends could do. By God's grace, we'll be friends for life! You know who you are!

Out of the Fowler's Snare

Psalm 124:2-8

If the Lord had not been on (my) side
when men attacked (me),
when their anger flared against (me),
they would have swallowed (me) alive;
the flood would have engulfed (me),
the torrent would have swept over (me),
the raging waters
would have swept (me) away.
Praise be to the Lord,
Who has not let (me) be torn
by their teeth.
(I) have escaped like a bird
out of the fowler's snare;
The snare has been broken,
and (I) have escaped.
(My) help is in the name of the Lord,
the maker of heaven and earth.

Part 1

The Capture

Chapter 1

It's strange, but it never really occurred to me that I was ugly until my sophomore year of high school. I was born the third child in a family of seven children. Our family was always more than a bit out of the norm. Because we had a larger than average family for the early 1960s, we needed a "mansion" to house us all. My parents were rather outspoken Christians and always witnessing about Jesus Christ to acquaintances and strangers alike. We were unusual in the sense that we went to church on more than just Sunday mornings. We went Sunday nights and Wednesdays, too. To some people, that was weird. My youngest brother was born with Down's syndrome, so that set all of us apart as a bit odd. My mom struggled with her weight after her seventh baby, and my dad had a glass eye replacing the one he had lost as a young man. In many ways I knew that our family was different, but we were a loving and close family unit. We stuck together and looked out for each other as needed. As kids, we fought like cats and dogs, but only with each other. Against others, we joined forces, as it should be.

We were all quite smart and for the most part did very well in school. Even my brother with Down's was considered very intelligent for a child with this syndrome. School was a breeze! I liked school, and by second grade thought maybe I'd become a teacher. Of course, at that time, most girls were going to be teachers, nurses, or moms at home. I had many friends at school. We did all the girlie things together like trading shoes (my saddle shoes for Patty's patent leather ones), playing Chinese jump rope, chasing and fighting with boys, going to slumber parties, and whispering about the secrets of growing up. I had many friends around me and felt like I fit in just fine.

I can't say that I felt like a beautiful princess, but it never occurred to me to feel ugly. My parents never really encouraged us toward beauty. In fact, wearing makeup and having the latest fad styles were frowned upon. Practicality, the economics of having a large family, and my parents' Christian beliefs kept all of that in check. I remember my dad telling me I was average in looks, when I so badly wanted him to tell me I was gorgeous. I guess he was just being truthful and didn't want me to have an unrealistic view of myself. I wanted to be gorgeous, but I decided I must be just OK. Definitely not ugly.

My life was happy and fairly carefree. My mom was always the more serious caregiver, while Dad was usually accused of just giving us the "fun times." My dad's boyhood family had worked hard, but then they enjoyed life, traveling and touring, winters in Texas, and playing games with family and friends. My dad wanted to give his own kids some of those same joys, minus the winters in Texas. We had ponies and dogs, Friday family game nights, ice cream cones on the way home from church, vacations to many of the national parks and tourist attractions of our great country, Sunday walks down the railroad tracks, and a lot of laughter in our mansion on the hill. My mom, because of her stern, hard-working German heritage, was more serious in her parenting. She thought children should be seen, and not heard, and have clean fingernails for church, which was kind of a joke with seven of us. Even when she was exhausted by the effort, she made sure we were always clean, well-pressed, well-fed, and prayed over before she sent us out the door for school. She was a good and godly mom who taught us much, including that life was not just about the fun times.

Because I was clean, wrinkle-free, and smart, my teachers and classmates thought well of me. My grades were good, my behavior mostly good, and the fighting at school was minimal. (I saved that for home with my many siblings and for the annoyance of my mom.) On one or two occasions, a girl in my class tried to call me a name that would indicate I was maybe just a bit ugly. I set her straight in a hurry by offering her my fist if she wanted to come a bit closer and say it again. I knew I was OK, definitely not ugly.

Chapter 2

There is a time for everything,
and a season for every activity under heaven...
Ecclesiastes 3:1 [NIV]

As my friends and I moved in the direction of puberty, of course, there was a lot more whispering about the mysteries of growing up. The world was beginning to change greatly in the late 1960s, but it took a while to trickle down to our community and neighborhood. We pretty much still whispered about such things.

At school, we couldn't help but notice that we had a handsome new principal to lead us. He had played football on the city team, held a record for the longest return for a touchdown, and was blond and young. How could we not take notice?

But, there was something else very different about him. He started a fellowship group of Christian athletes in our school and a young people's fellowship group in his home on Sunday nights. My parents encouraged the three oldest of us, still at home, to go and see what it was all about. We liked it and kept going each Sunday night. We soaked in the biblical teachings and respected the leadership of our principal and his wife. I especially took notice of, and had crushes on, some of the athletes who also attended. Life was good and life was sweet.

Along with the general feelings of happiness, I was beginning to grow spiritually. It was no longer that I just had Christian parents, I wanted to be a "Jesus Freak", too. Having a handsome principal who was bold about his faith made it easier to be confident about mine. It's sort of amazing to look back now and see how bold I was becoming in my faith. I carried my Bible to school with me each day. Although this seems weird in retrospect, I even put Jesus stickers on the buttons of my spring coat. Of course, having a Christian principal, who was also carrying his Bible each day helped give me courage. This was before the American Civil Liberties Union (ACLU), and others, became more aggressive in wanting all mention of God and faith removed from the public schools, and society in general.

My mom also encouraged having a personal time for Bible reading and prayer at that time in my life. She said I was old enough to start doing that on my own. Through the Sunday night fellowship group and my own devotional time, I started to become more curious and interested in the Holy Spirit's role in my life. I went so far as to invite Him into my life and asked Him to show Himself to me. He was faithful to do that in a big and meaningful way.

Looking back, I realize that God knew I would need His Spirit for the treacherous road ahead of me. Sometimes I feel mad that God knew what was ahead and didn't prevent it. Other times, I feel grateful knowing that He knew and gave me what I would need to actually survive it.

Chapter 3

During my junior high years, I became more and more interested in horses and boys. My parents encouraged my love of horses and didn't worry too much about the boy thing. Once in a while the horse thing and the boy thing would intersect, which was delightful and exciting, but very innocent and of no real parental concern.

My dad was able to support a family of nine by working hard as a real estate broker. He loved his work and provided well for his large family. As a broker, various properties would cross his desk and occasionally he would show an interest in moving out of the mansion on the hill.

The fact that we lived in the mansion on the hill was because of his real estate business. He and his business partner decided to develop a subdivision of homes on what had been an old farmstead. It was called April Hill. One of the main drives up the hill was given our last name. That just added to the view that our family was out of the ordinary but in a good way. As a kid, I thought that was very cool to have a road named after us. As they were developing the land for new homes, certain covenants and ordinances were set down for the legal record.

Within a short time, a handful of new homes had been built on the hill. It seemed that everyone who moved in wanted to have horses or ponies for their children. My dad and his partner were generous with the unsold and empty lots, and pretty soon there was a variety of horse paddocks, simple sheds, and pastures scattered around the hill.

Our family started out with two ill-mannered ponies named Rusty and Dusty. They didn't last too long. Then Tinker Belle, Queenie, and Pal joined our extended family. Tinker Belle was mine and very well loved. Life just got better and better as we spent our days with the horses and the other neighborhood kids.

It was a rude awakening when a family moved in next door to us that did not like horses and did not want one for their children. How could that be? All of a sudden, the legal land-use covenants became an issue.

It was a heart-breaking thing for all of us horse lovers in the neighborhood. We were told that the horses needed to be moved by a certain date. I thought that since my dad started the subdivision and our road was named after us, surely we wouldn't have to get rid of our horses. But, no, my dad had helped to write the covenants, and they were legal, and our horses would need to go, too.

It was devastating to a young girl's heart, but my dad would find a way to make it right. For a short time, we were able to board our horses at a neighboring farm, provided they could share the sheep pen. Before long, my dad had a longer range plan worked out. He bought an old farm in a different town. The house just needed to be gutted and rebuilt to make it livable. Plumbing and electricity would need to be added, too. But, at least it had a barn, pastures, a small indoor arena, and other outbuildings. My dad was thrilled about being able to give his kids not only their horses, but all kinds of life experiences on a farm. We would still be a close and loving family but just in a new location in a new town. We kids started to dream and plan for what it would actually be like to live on a farm with plenty of space and buildings for the horses. We had many months to wait as the house was updated to a livable condition. That gave my older brother time to graduate from high school with his class. I was able to finish out my freshman year of high school and say my farewells to my many close friends. We knew it wasn't good-bye. I was already planning to come back for all of the Friday night football games and the Sunday night fellowship. It would be fine. We just wouldn't see each other every day at school. I'd be able to keep Tinker Belle, and everything would be great. Or so I thought...

Chapter 4

It was during the summer of my fifteenth year when we moved to the farm. We kids, and dad, too, were very excited. Mom probably wasn't as excited because, of course, it was a lot of work to move nine people out of the mansion and onto the farm. I wanted to enjoy my summer and wasn't too worried about the school year ahead. I knew there would be new friends to make, but it would be fine, when the time came.

Summer rushed quickly by, and on an August day my mom said it was time to go register for school. I felt nervous about the whole process, but I guessed it had to be done. I would be the only one of my family to go to the high school that year. My three younger sisters would be going to the elementary and middle schools that fall. Our youngest brother would be going to special education classes nearby.

Once the formalities and paperwork were completed, there was nothing else to do but wait for my new adventure in my new school. I was smart, had Christian faith, had been well liked by my teachers, had many friends at my old school, had OK looks, and was clean and well-pressed. I had no doubt that things would be comfortable for me within a few days.

The first day of school started with an uneasy bus ride into town, but at least I had my three sisters sharing the experience. Soon they were dropped off at their respective schools, and I was alone on the journey to my new high school. I told myself everything would be fine. It would just be a little scary for a day or two until I found my way around and made some new friends.

As luck would have it, I met another new girl just starting her sophomore year in our new school. She was a military "brat" who had gone to school in Germany the previous year. She was cute, laughed easily, and carried the possibility of a new friendship for me on that first day of school. Day One went reasonably well, but even so, I couldn't wait to get home and get out for a nice long ride on Tinker Belle to clear my head!

The second day of school came quickly and with it a sense of dark foreboding. My new friend came with some unbelievable news. Yesterday after school, her older brother told her that other students in school thought his sister was ugly and were referring to her with a repulsive name—Largemouth Bass. She felt badly, and I felt badly for her, too. I thought she was cute and in no way looked at all like a fish or any other ugly creature. She had no need to worry. I would still be her friend.

By the middle of that day, the clouded picture became much clearer. It seemed the new girl they were referring to and ridiculing was not his sister and my new friend, but me. She was greatly relieved, and I was devastated. It was only the beginning of what would become a dark and lonely downward spiral. My sense that all was well with the world, and with me, was brutally shattered.

As I heard the whisperings of "largemouth bass" through the day, I felt terrible shame and humiliation. It didn't take long for my newly acquired friend to put some distance between herself and me, the ugly new girl. I felt very alone and couldn't believe this was happening to me. Nothing like it had ever happened before! My tormentors didn't seem to even care if I heard their words, or if teachers heard what they were saying. I felt so embarrassed! What must my new teachers think of me? By the time the dismissal bell rang on Day Two, I was full of relief and uncried tears as I boarded my bus for home. I didn't say a word to my sisters about what had happened to me at school. They seemed happy enough about their days. As quickly as I was able to get into my grubby jeans, I was out with Tinker Belle, sharing with her my unspoken grief.

My heart was breaking in a way that I had never experienced before. I did not want anyone to know what others were saying about me. It was a dark secret that I was afraid to tell even to my parents. I thought they loved me, but what if they agreed with what the kids were saying? Maybe I was hideously ugly and looked like a largemouth bass. That's not something a parent could tell their child, but maybe they would think it in their minds. I, for sure, did not want my sisters to know, because I knew they would use it against me, as siblings will in the heat of battle. It was a heavy, dark, shameful secret and one that I would need to bear alone—for many years to come.

Tinker Belle gave some brief respite from the pain. I couldn't even voice my brokenness to her with spoken words. But, she must have sensed the grief as I leaned into her and felt the warm moist breath from her muzzle on my hands and face. I was absolutely wracked with turmoil and grief, but I didn't often allow the tears to flow, and certainly not when anyone could see or hear me. The burden seemed to be mine to bear alone. Somehow I was hoping that it was all a mistake and that it would blow over in a few days or weeks.

Chapter 5

God! Why? Please don't let them say it! Please, God, in the Name of Jesus, please don't let them say it. Please! I beg You! How many times each school day did I agonizingly plead that within my soul? On rare occasions, God seemed to be merciful and kept my torturers at bay, but more often than not, the painful words were shouted down the hall or whispered behind my back in the lunch line. Each day was filled with continuing reminders of just how very ugly I was. Is there anything on the planet uglier than a largemouth bass?

The faith that had grown in me over the previous few years was still there along with the Jesus stickers on my coat buttons. I did carry my Bible with me for at least a few days as I started my new school year, but as the torturous ridicule became more intense, I found that I lost all boldness to stand out for my faith. In fact, I just wanted to blend into the woodwork and have nobody notice me at all. I didn't want anyone to even see me, but it seemed they could, and they let everyone else know when the Largemouth Bass was anywhere nearby.

I knew I was a Christian in my heart, but I began to bury that secret within me. I didn't want to stand out as different in yet another way. And besides, where was God in all this pain? Why wasn't He coming to my rescue? Did He see what was happening? Did He hear the intentional hurtful words being thrown at me? Did He even care about how my heart was being ripped apart each day? Did He see how I was carrying the pain alone, not even telling the people who loved me the most? Did He even hear my agonized prayers?

Relief rushed over me each day when the school bus finally dropped me off at home. In a few minutes I would be out with Tinker Belle, who provided me with sweet reprieve after another horrendous day at school. She was my main source of comfort in the daily and lonely pain.

As planned and promised before our big move to the farm, I was sometimes able to go back to my old school for the Friday night football and basketball games. It was such a joy to see and spend time with kind and faithful friends from my old life. They didn't seem to see that I looked like a largemouth bass. They just knew me as Roseanne. I could be with friends, and hide from those who hunted me, for a few safe Friday night hours.

My parents also decided that if my older brother was willing to drive us, we could still attend the Sunday night fellowship group. We did, and usually got home quite late for the school day ahead. The huge moan on Monday morning was only partially from lack of sleep. It was more a whimper of dread for the day and another week ahead at school. The brief relief from the ridicule was over.

Chapter 6

How many ways are there to let a person know that you think they are hideous and look like a largemouth bass? I'm not sure. But, it seemed like an endless number.

The favorite way seemed to be to holler it down the main hallways if I was anywhere nearby. It didn't matter if you were even in my class of sophomores or not. The upper classmen, who really should have had better things to do, joined in the fun, too. The freshmen were just glad it wasn't them as the target of the joke. "Largemouth Bass, Largemouth Bass!" I wish I could give you an idea of how it sounded in print form, but that is not possible. The words were shouted in a loud, derisive, sneering kind of way that took the hurtful words way beyond their own literal meaning and added the element of total disgust for the victim. Me.

That was the preferred way of showing contempt for the new girl, but other ways served the purpose, too. Just whispering the words Largemouth Bass behind my back in class or in the lunch line brought total embarrassment and humiliation to me. And, they knew it. The ring of their laughter only accentuated my shame.

It seemingly provided even more glee for my tormentors when a teacher would take notice of what they were saying. Not that the teachers ever joined in. I don't believe they did, and in fact, they were probably at a loss as to what they should do to rescue the new girl. (This was long before the Columbine shootings and any talk of the consequences of bullying in schools.) At least one teacher would respond to their teasing with, "Did you say you were a largemouth bass?" Everyone got a huge laugh out of that, except for me who was cringing in the corner, just dying for biology to be over. Forever.

I suppose I could be grateful for their direct and honest evaluation of my looks. The most painful ridicule really was given more subtly. It was dealt out in shadowy nuances, puns, and side jokes relative to anything "fishy". One example was when our French class was going to have a celebratory party. It was noted that the "LMB" could provide the caviar for the party. How humiliating to have those words actually spoken aloud about me, in front of Madame, our teacher. Besides the fish connotation, there seemed to be a sexual aspect to it, as well. Everyone knew who the LMB was, and caviar is fish eggs from the female. Poor Madame was clueless as to what she might say to defend me. I never held it against her. I think, had she said anything to shield me, it would have only made things worse in some way or another.

I suppose I should have been happy that Largemouth Bass was occasionally shortened to LMB, but somehow the sting was the same whether the actual words or initials were used. It didn't matter. An ugly fish is still an ugly fish. Everyone knew who I was, and it couldn't be denied.

Chapter 7

One may ask, as I have asked myself hundreds of times, do I look like a largemouth bass? Prior to moving to my new school, I had never considered the fact that I looked anything but OK, not beautiful, but certainly not ugly either. My schoolmates and friends at my old school never told me I looked like a fish.

After hearing the openly sarcastic words being thrown at me, I was forced to look at myself in a whole new way. Did I look like a largemouth bass? Of course, I had to furtively locate a picture of one so I even knew what they looked like. I had gone fishing many times with my dad and brother, but I never thought much about how a fish looked. Fishing was for fun and for sport in good company. I never thought of a fish as being the ugliest form of life on the planet. Now, I was beginning to learn and know better.

After seeing an encyclopedic picture of what a largemouth bass looked like, I spent a good deal of secret time in front of the bathroom mirror trying to determine if I did, indeed, look like a fish. I could see that my actual mouth was wide like my mom's, and my lower lip was quite full like my dad's. It seemed that my top lip was less full and maybe a little crooked, again, like my mom's. What cruel act of nature conspired to give me the worst of both parents? I also had been a thumb-sucker for too many years, which probably also distorted the shape of my mouth.

In my continuing behind-closed-doors assessment of my looks, I mulled over my baby pictures for signs of ugliness or a fish-like look. The pictures didn't seem to match with what the kids at school were saying about me. I thought I was a cute baby. My eyes were bright and sparkly. But, maybe I did have an extra wide smile. Could that have turned into a fishy look, as I got older?

Every teenager has heard from their parents or teachers that young people go through a time of awkwardness as their bodies change and mature. Maybe feet or noses grow too fast, but eventually everything catches up and equalizes. Teens are told not to worry about such things. Were my fish lips an example of this?

After much private personal evaluation, I determined that when I smiled and laughed, I actually had a very pretty mouth, but when I didn't hold my mouth in a smile, maybe it did look just a little ugly. But, did I look like a largemouth bass? Maybe. I tried not to accept that about myself, but when you are repeatedly told that on a daily basis every school day of the year, it becomes increasingly difficult to persuade yourself that what others are saying is not true.

Consequently, it seemed to me that the solution to my problem was that I just needed to always hold my mouth in a smile. If I always smiled, I wouldn't look like that dreadful fish. That sounded good in theory; however, it never worked for long. As soon as the daily ridicule and bullying started, the corners of my mouth immediately dropped down, and no amount of self-talk could make me put on a smile. My heart was being ripped apart one damaging word at a time, and there was no way I could even fake a smile. I wanted to die, or at least disappear. There was no possible way for me to force a smile. With each cutting criticism, the corners of my mouth dropped into a deeper frown. In my sadness, I probably was beginning to look like a largemouth bass, with my down-turned mouth.

On occasion, various bullies would throw in other hurtful words, reflective of how they thought I looked, like lizard or duck. Those names must have had less impact or brought less laughter, because they always returned to the choice morsel of Largemouth Bass.

I fought hard to keep from accepting the fact that I was ugly. No longer just not pretty, not even OK, but just plain ugly. No, I was worse than ugly. Day in and day out, I was reminded of how very repulsive I was. It was only a matter of time before I bought the lie...hook, line, and sinker.

Chapter 8

Through the torment, I was not totally without friends in my new school. I had two very compassionate friends that were obviously concerned for the new "loser" of their sophomore class. Without them, God alone knows if I would have survived.

One of them was Lori, the daughter of a local minister. She was petite and cute, and at least, not disliked by most of our classmates. She seemed somewhat oblivious to what they thought of her, anyway, and just lived her life to her own drumbeat.

The other was Sharon, a perky, freckled friend bound to a wheelchair for life. She had a wild streak and was well-liked by most of the class. Her wheelchair limited her physically but not from fun and partying with her class.

Lori was a friend to Sharon and could often be seen wheeling her from class to class. Outside of school, as petite as Lori was, she would toss that heavy wheelchair into the trunk of her car and race off for some onion rings with Sharon in tow.

I don't recollect exactly how they befriended me, but all of a sudden, I wasn't totally alone. I was still in deep and torturous emotional pain, but at least I had two friends. My parents were happy to see that I had formed some friendships and assumed that things were going just fine at my new school. I never told them anything that would lead them to believe other than that.

Not only did I never speak to my parents or siblings about my painful situation, I never spoke of it with Lori and Sharon. It seems a shame that it was never brought up between us. They obviously knew exactly how I was being treated and probably befriended me out of compassion for my situation. It wasn't a secret to them. They saw it daily, too. I think if I could have talked to them about my pain and how ugly and degraded I was feeling, maybe they could have offered me some comfort. But, I never brought it up, and neither did they. It was like a massive elephant in the living room that we all lived our lives around but never mentioned. Shouldn't one of us have brought up the stench of that elephant? But, we didn't. So although I wasn't without a friend, I was still very alone in my heart and mind.

I thought that after my newness wore off, maybe my tormentors would just leave me alone and move on to someone else to pick on. I could hope, couldn't I?

Sharon and Lori were both good students who generally maintained excellent grades in school. During our sophomore year, we were beginning to think and talk about our futures. All three of us wanted to go to college and become either special education teachers or physical therapists. The compassion of my two friends extended not only to me but to anyone in need of a helping hand.

As we talked about our plans for college, the topic of grade point averages, valedictorian status, and graduation speeches came up in conversation. Although unvoiced, I decided then and there, that there was NO WAY I would want to have a grade point average high enough to be given the opportunity to stand up in front of my class for any reason. I felt absolute horror at the possibility of my parents observing my very public ridicule at the graduation ceremony. I determined that my grades must be lowered so that no possibility could exist of that very public outing of the Largemouth Bass.

Chapter 9

Even though graduation was still a few years away, I began to plot out how to avoid having a high ranking in my graduating class. I had always done so well in school with relative ease. Now I had to figure out a way to make sure that I would never be considered for giving a speech on my last day of high school. I began to sabotage my "permanent record".

I had always loved science and was taking both biology and chemistry. In the early 1970s, calculators were expensive and rare even for the average adult. Students didn't have them, so we were learning how to do all of our calculations using a slide rule. I found it somewhat challenging but within the realm of my ability. I decided not to worry too much about my grades and to let them fall where they may. I thought that if I made a C grade in chemistry, I would definitely not be giving a speech at graduation.

Unfortunately, the chemistry teacher must have known that my grades were not lining up with what he expected of this new sophomore transplant. He must have known that I was bright and capable, but my grades weren't looking that way.

One fateful Friday, the teacher had me come up to the chalkboard at the front of the room. He gave me a problem and asked me to solve it for the class. He would not let me sit down until I solved the problem. I stood there for the remainder of the class period appearing quite clueless about how to find the solution. To this point in time, I had been more concerned about my grades being too high rather than learning the strategies that I needed to master. Not only did I appear clueless; I probably was quite clueless. What he did was humiliating to me. I was already a despised standout in my new school. To have to stand up in front of my chemistry classmates for an extended time made it that much worse. By the time the period bell rang, I think I almost crawled out of the class in embarrassment.

Truthfully, I don't think this educator's intent was to be cruel. I think he simply knew that I was capable, but not performing. Amazingly, I never held it against him, or at least for long.

The extended disgrace must have made a huge impression on me. That weekend, I went home and sequestered myself in my bedroom until I had mastered the slide rule and all the possible chemistry problems that could spring up on me. I determined that he would not be able to shame me ever again.

Even though the students may have isolated me, this teacher was never unkind to me after that. In fact, I was only one of a few students who continued on with him for advanced chemistry.

As far as undermining my own grade-point average, I decided that I needed to be more subtle about it than I had been in chemistry class. Be a good student, just not too good. I remember my mom questioning those A- and B+ grades. I never gave her a clue about the real reason why I was not maintaining the coveted 4.0 G.P.A. She would have been deeply heartsick if she had only known the truth.

I should note that as my sisters reached the end of their high school careers, two of them were the valedictorians of their graduating classes. I believe one sister ranked third. In retrospect, I know that I could have experienced their same level of success had I not purposely avoided it. In some ways, that leaves me feeling incredibly sad. But, at the time, it seemed my only option. I was holding a dark and ugly secret within me. I just couldn't let my parents know my truth.

Chapter 10

I continued to live with dread for each day of the school year. I fumbled along in misery praying that something would change. It wasn't that I wanted to all of a sudden be popular or even acceptable; I just wanted to fade into the woodwork and be left alone. If I could have just drifted invisibly through my day, that would have been fine with me. (A few years later when making my college decision, one of my primary considerations was the number of students enrolled and if I would be able to "fade into the woodwork." Although my parents didn't really know why, that became my motto.)

I desperately wanted God to do something about my circumstances. But no amount of begging, pleading, bargaining, or private tears seemed to make a difference. I prayed repeatedly through my day that I would not be called on by the teachers.

Even in the English classes that I loved, I would sit uneasily through the period, hoping not to get called on for any reason. I had superior reading skills, but when I was called on to read aloud, it was as if my throat would close up. I actually had trouble breathing. I would repeatedly attempt to clear my throat enough to be heard, but rarely was I able to read in a relaxed and fluent way. I hated being put in the spotlight even for something that I would have normally enjoyed.

It was probably difficult for my teachers to have me truly academically engaged and yet not ever put me at the center of attention. Any half-conscious teacher had to have known my plight. A discerning and compassionate teacher must surely have felt my pain, too. (I can only imagine the conversations in the inner sanctum of the teachers' lounge!)

For the most part I liked my teachers. I knew they were just doing their jobs. A teacher had to occasionally call on a student to check for understanding. It was a normal part of any class to have to read and discuss the topics aloud. Many of my teachers tried to make it OK for me, but it just wasn't OK no matter what they did.

Had it not been for my dark and ugly secret, I would have truly enjoyed school and my teachers. Prior to moving to this new town, most of my school experiences were positive, and even the normal ups and downs of school life could be viewed in a humorous way. Now, there was nothing humorous about my daily life.

As I said, during that first year after the big move, my sisters were not yet in the high school. They were still in elementary and middle school. We did share a common bus ride before and after school that year. I am unsure whether they picked up on the ridicule of their big sister or not. If they did, they never acknowledged it to me. We never spoke of it. (Again, I bore my shame alone!)

It is not that my sisters never teased me or picked on me. They certainly did, as many siblings do, but they never used the most painful of words—largemouth bass. My one sister occasionally called me "squinty pig eyes" when she was really mad at me, but the sting of that was mild compared to what the other option would have been. (We laugh about her name for me now. She has no idea why she chose to call me that. We have considered that maybe I squinted when I didn't wear my glasses.)

Each day, as I stepped off that school bus at home, relief flooded over me. It just washed over me—especially if it happened to be on a Friday afternoon. With the weekend came two days of relative calm in the eye of the week-to-week storms.

Chapter 11

My family did most of their business and activity beyond the borders of our new small town. Thank God! The main exception was in filling the car with gasoline. That was back in the day of full-service gas stations, since self-serve stations were a new and rare option in the early 1970s.

As my mom pulled into one of the corner full-service gas stations I would be cringing and cowering on the inside, if not visibly on the outside, as one of my classmates or an upper classman came out to pump our gas. He would lean down to look in the window, maybe give a smirky smile, but say nothing cruel in front of my mom. God!?!?

I would disconnectedly endure the pumping of the gasoline and the cleaning of the windshield. Wouldn't you know it, he would ask my mom if she'd like the oil checked. Yes, that would be fine—and if the oil level was low, I'd have to wait further while he added a quart. Then my mom, making matters almost unbearable for me, would attempt to be a faithful witness for her Lord. If there was no one waiting in line for fuel services, she would begin to ask him about his faith or if he went to church in town. By that time I was about ready to crawl, no—slither, out of the car and find a hiding spot. By the time the "Have a nice day," was said, my day felt beyond fixable.

Not a word was spoken to me, or about me, by the attendant. It was the unspoken words that were eating me up. The unspoken words in my head, and the realization that he probably would have liked to have said them, but only out of deference to an adult and a paying customer had he held his tongue. I was really glad he did! I wouldn't have wanted to talk about this with my mom, not that day, or ever.

Other infrequent business in the town included quick stops at the local grocery store or maybe the root beer stand. I'm sure my parents had no comprehension of why the local grocery store should be such a dreaded place for me.

Later, when I became a licensed driver, my parents frequently asked me to pick up groceries for the family. I would usually drive an extra 20 minutes (and back) to go to a grocery store in the neighboring city. They didn't ask many questions of me as long as the chore was completed.

A stop at the local root beer stand should have been a treat, but in reality it wasn't. I was always comforted when we just quickly picked up a gallon jug of cold root beer to take home instead of eating a meal with carhop service. Although most of the carhops were teen girls, and most of my tormentors were boys, I never felt like I could let down my guard in the presence of any kids from my high school. I didn't want any bad surprises, and especially not in front of my siblings or parents. Just get me out of town in a hurry! Relief came rolling in with each mile as we headed toward our home in the country.

Chapter 12

In the Bible, Psalm 33:17 says, "A horse is a vain hope for deliverance; despite all its great strength it cannot save." Maybe not, but in many ways, my little horse Tinker Belle was a large piece of my salvation during those years. If it hadn't been for her, I don't think I could have found the strength to go on living my high school life. She was the one living, breathing, touchable being that I trusted with my pain. It didn't seem that God was responding or even seeing my hurt at that time, but Tinker Belle was always there for me. She would greet me with a welcoming whinny as the school bus ground to a halt at the top of our driveway. She gave accepting, unconditional love, as animals are known to do. She didn't care whether I looked like a largemouth bass or a lizard. She didn't seem to be concerned that I was ugly.

With my eyes downcast and my heart bleeding on the inside from the school day, I hurried to my bedroom to dump off my books and grab my dusty, horse-hair-covered jeans. Only as I ran to faithful Tinker Belle did the pent-up emotions of the day begin to slowly seep out of me. Small measures of comfort came as I brushed and patted her warm coat. Even shoveling the unending manure made me breathe more peacefully. Many days I was able to take a quiet ride before the demands of my other chores, both inside the house and out, brought me back to reality.

I realize now that I was like an old-fashioned pressure cooker. Being with Tinker Belle was my release valve that allowed me to return to school each day and take the bullying for just one more day. Day after day, I barely hung on. I don't think I could have ever looked beyond that single day. If I had, it would have been unbearable. Life already seemed on the brink of unendurable, but I just determined to hold on for another school day. When, and if, I could no longer hold on, I would come up with a plan to end my pain. I was surviving (not living) life just one single school day at a time.

When I say that God didn't seem to be there for me or even be aware of my suffering, I know now that wasn't the truth. Maybe even at the time I knew that wasn't the truth, but that was my emotionally-perceived view of the truth. I couldn't touch Him physically, I couldn't hear Him with my physical ears, and when I cried out to Him, it seemed that nobody was hearing my cries. I believed He was out there somewhere, all-knowing and all-powerful, but apparently not concerned with what I was going through at school. I believed that He was able to intervene on my behalf, but He didn't, even when I repeatedly begged Him for help.

A godly person might say that this high-school ordeal was His will for my life and something that He allowed to happen to me. This same person might say that nothing happens to God's children without it passing through His hands. In days-long-past satan himself (lower-case intended) couldn't torment the God-fearing man Job without asking God for permission. Obviously, God must have allowed it to happen to me, because it did happen.

So many times I have been thankful for my little horse Tinker Belle, who helped me survive day to day. But as I think about her, I also acknowledge that if it hadn't been for her and our other horses we would have never been forced to move out of our mansion on April Hill. We would have never gone to a new high school in a new town with new kids to meet. I probably would have never been emotionally bullied to the point of considering ending my life. I possibly may have continued my relatively carefree and happy life and finished high school with many friends and a valedictory speech. But, it was not to be.

In my wonderings, I have asked if Tinker Belle was the catalyst or the provision for my pain. I haven't come to a verdict on that, even decades later. Was God keenly aware that a horse could help a young girl survive an extended crisis and enable her to hang on for just one more day? Did He provide Tinker Belle as a tangible and touchable source of comfort in the physical realm? Maybe He saw it all ahead of time and had made this provision for my survival as a means of His intervention. He didn't rescue me and take me out of the pain, but maybe, just maybe, He used a horse to save me from destruction.

My dad bought Tinker Belle for me when I was about eleven years old. I wanted a horse to take as a 4-H project. My dad, always wanting to give his kids good gifts, thought that would be a fine idea. From my strong point of view, I thought it should be a beautiful young Appaloosa with a subtly-spotted blanket of white on a mostly warm-brown body. I wanted her name to be Frosted Fawn. I just knew in my heart that I could train her to be a winner.

It was maddening at the time, but an experienced older gentleman working with the 4-H horse projects advised my dad against my view of the perfect horse. He told my dad that a young, inexperienced rider and a young, inexperienced horse were not a good combination. At age eleven I was sure he didn't know what he was talking about. My dad saw the wisdom of it and asked the horseman to help him find a good horse for his daughter. It took a few months, but he located an 8-year-old, well-behaved mare named Tinker Belle. She wasn't Frosted Fawn, but I soon fell deeply in love with her.

The 4-H horse program proved to be an emotionally safe and wonderful experience for me until the autumn that I left for college. Kids that loved horses were apparently a breed apart from the average high school student. Not once was I ridiculed or made to feel inferior about my looks while attending 4-H functions or horse shows. It was one setting where I could be present and not feel on my guard waiting to be ridiculed. In truth, I probably was very much on my guard, but the teasing never came. It may have helped that the 4-H club that we joined after the move was in a neighboring town and not in the town where I went to high school. In any case,

4-H provided me with something I loved, in a place of safety.

Chapter 13

The reader may question, "Where in the world were your parents during this time? Why didn't they see your pain and come to your rescue? Could they have been totally oblivious to what you were going through?" Truthfully, I don't know how they could not have seen my pain because I was so intensely filled with it. It's hard to understand how they could have missed it. We've all heard the tales of even psychopathic students going on shooting rampages in their schools, and the parents seemingly had no idea that their children were having issues at school.

It would do the reader well to remember that I was determined not to let my parents or siblings know about what was happening at school. I didn't want them to find out lest maybe they would agree with the verdict of my school peers and find me to be incredibly ugly, too. In hindsight, it seems so sad to think that I didn't trust their love enough to know better. It was obviously a lie that I believed in my mind. My parents would have loved me and supported me in any way that they could.

Besides the doubts and wonderings about whether they might agree with the opinions of my schoolmates, I was a little afraid of how my parents might back me up. Would my mom go marching into the principal's office wondering about why her daughter was being picked on at school? Would she make a scene? Would it just make things worse for me on all accounts? Would word get back to the perpetrators that my mom had come in to defend me? Then the real torment would begin, plus the principal would have to take notice of me, too. There was NO WAY I wanted any of those things to happen.

I had at least one past experience that led me to believe that it wouldn't be a good idea for my mom to come to my defense, no matter what. She occasionally joked about being a mother bear willing to come to the aid of her cubs. That might be fine in nature but not in the public schools. Not my mom, for sure, and not to my defense.

I clearly remembered one time when my mom did call the school about a bus driver inappropriately touching the young girls on the bus, including my youngest sister. Honestly, my mom was very right in making the call, and it probably took some courage to pick up the phone to speak with the principal. Today child sexual abuse is more publicly spoken of and is often a feature on the local evening news. Back in the early 1970s it was still a shocking thought that people didn't much talk about publicly. These days the bus driver would no doubt face arrest, charges, and loss of his job, but that was not the consequence then. If anything, he may have been joked about in terms of being a dirty old man. It's good that these types of offenses to children are taken more seriously at this time in our history. They've always happened. It's just that people are now more willing to speak of such abuses publicly.

After my mom made the call, the word came down the line from the principal to the dirty old man, to the other kids on the bus, and then to us, that our mom had complained about his behavior. We kids ended up being the ones teased because our mom had the nerve to call and try to protect her child and the other young girls on the bus. The bus driver never received any punishment, other than maybe a warning to keep his hands to himself, but then proceeded to let everyone know our mom had reported him. At least he kept his hands off my sister after that. However, the lesson learned by the kids in our family was, "Don't tell Mom." We didn't want that to happen again and at times made a verbal plea and pact with each other to make sure it didn't. I'm not implying my mom shouldn't have come to our defense. I'm just saying that from a kid's point of view there were reasons you wouldn't want your mom to know.

Another factor in my parents not realizing my pain was just the fact that there were seven of us children in the family. Life was incredibly busy and full of semi-organized chaos. The care and time demands made by my brother with Down's syndrome went well beyond the needs of an average child. Remember, my mom was trying to keep us all well-fed, clean, pressed, and prayed for each day. Truthfully, I think my mom lived her life in a perpetual state of exhaustion, as many mothers do.

My dad also worked long hours to help run the household and to support his family financially. When he wasn't physically at his downtown office he was frequently working in his home office. Many nights after the family dinner, his work day extended into the evening. Although disputed by my mother, he was very involved in parenting his children and helping to keep the household running smoothly. He helped with bedtime routines, hanging laundry, and buying groceries. After moving to the farm he supervised all of the outdoor animal chores.

In many ways my parents might have been living life one day at a time and just trying to survive, too, like me. When they would ask me if everything was OK or if there was anything bothering me, I always said things were fine. More than likely they didn't have the time or energy to pursue the question any further. They probably hoped and prayed that I was fine and then moved on to the next pressing responsibility. They never really knew the truth of my daily situation.

In my writing of this book I have been guarded in letting my parents know too much or even read any pages to this point. They would be very grieved by my pain, knowing that they weren't there for me when I was in need. We have occasionally talked about my not liking the new school and being "picked on", but in very general terms. They have expressed sorrow in not knowing and in not helping me, but they really don't know the specific details revealed in this book. I think it would be too painful for them to read what really happened to me in my own words. I don't hold them culpable for their not being there for me. They just didn't know, and I didn't want them to know. Who's to blame for that?

Chapter 14

With early June came the end of my sophomore year at the new high school. Could it still be called new after nine full months? (For me, it would always be the new high school.) The daily and constant derision had lasted my entire sophomore year, and by then the damage to my psyche was complete.

The school year wrapped up with a sigh heard 'round the world, or so it seemed to me. My relief was tangible, knowing that my torment was mostly over for the summer. I was looking forward to three whole months of relief and hope. Sure, I knew it was possible that I could run into one or more of my tormentors, but we lived miles from town. I would make it a point not to go there any more than necessary and only when I had to with my parents.

With the summer warmth came many deliriously happy hours with Tinker Belle and the other horses. I was in the 4-H horse program and had two summer fairs to prepare for besides a few open horse shows that my parents were allowing me to enter. I loved every minute of the preparation because it allowed me to be hands-on with the horses for as many hours of the day as I wanted to be. Freedom from school and time with the horses—it didn't get much better than that from my point of view.

By this time, my dad was moving full-speed ahead in giving his family the "farmette" experience and loving every minute of it himself. Our menagerie now included miniature mules, cows, calves, goats, cats, dogs, pigs, and literally all types of poultry, including pheasants and peacocks. My dad loved the outdoor chores and had a large group of free laborers (his children) to help with them. Besides the horse chores I was expected to help with the two cows, Horns and Mama. I didn't mind, and it sure beat any indoor cleaning jobs that my mom might have in mind for me.

Even so, I was expected to help indoors just like everyone else in the family. Summer was a time to get done all the things that we couldn't get done during the school year. That meant there were always lists of job expectations for each child depending on our age and ability.

Besides the chores, this was my first summer as a young driver. I frequently begged my parents to take me out for some behind-the-wheel driving practice, and I finally scored my driver's license by early August. I was excited about that because I knew it would bring me more freedom. Without the structure of a school week I would have more time to drive myself back to see old friends. It was only about a thirty-five minute drive and my parents allowed me much liberty as long as I took care of my jobs around home first. The summer was filled with the chores of a large household and the joys of a young girl released from her torture chamber called high school.

I enjoyed each day fully, but I was ever conscious that the days of summer were flying by all too quickly. Although I did not want to waste a minute of this relatively happy time, I began to live in dread of the first day of my junior year of high school.

Chapter 15

As hard as I tried to dig my heels in and stop the passage of time, it didn't work. The end of August did eventually arrive with me cringing inside, shaking in my soon-to-be-set-aside cowgirl boots, and filled with anxiety. I was pretty sure that I knew what the first day would bring, but I was hoping against hope that somehow things might be different. Maybe being an upper-classman would somehow make things better. I did not want to go back to school, but I had no choice. It was expected of me, and I wasn't willing or able to explain my uneasy feelings to anyone. Even if I had been able to do so, homeschooling was basically unheard of in the early-1970s, and I'm sure my mother wouldn't have seriously considered it with all of her other responsibilities.

I truthfully don't remember my first day back to school as a junior, but I know that it wasn't long before the "largemouth bass" chorus started again. Because of the previous year, I was so damaged in my emotions and the view that I had of myself, that even if nobody had actually said it, I would have believed myself to be just an ugly LMB. I would have perceived, rightly or wrongly, the contempt—even if the words went unspoken.

In terms of frequency, things did improve just slightly during my junior year. The ridicule became less than daily and not quite so dependable. The downside of this "improvement" was that it flared up more randomly and unexpectedly. I never knew when I would be face-to-face with the rawness of it.

I was always guarded while at school or any related function. Because of this, I kept my school time to the absolute minimum that I could arrange. As juniors students are expected to get more involved with the clubs and activities of high school so they have something to show for themselves to future college admissions boards. Apparently the 4-H program and horse shows were not sufficient evidence of motivation for higher learning.

I tried to find things that could be done alone or with just one other person. One option was selling advertising for the school yearbook. Although I was really nervous about it, I went from business to business in town trying to sell advertising space for the annual Tomahawk. Most local business people were gracious and sympathetic towards us and willingly renewed their ads from the previous year.

The most uncomfortable part was the questions they had for me personally. They didn't recognize my last name as a local family name, so there were many questions to be answered about my family and me. This was exactly what I didn't want to talk about. With every question, I couldn't help wondering if they were seeing the largemouth bass in me, and what they were thinking of this new addition to their community. After each advertisement was sold I made a hurried get-away to my car. Most of the time my selling partner was faithful, dependable Lori. She made things only just tolerable for me.

Selling ads in the yearbook was not enough to get me into any respectable college. There had to be more that I could do to show my motivational drive, extracurricular talents, and school involvement. But what? The guidance counselor wanted to know the answer to this.

I finally agreed that I could work backstage for the school's theater production and presentation of *Brigadoon* (Alan Jay Lerner and Frederick Loewe), the Broadway musical made famous in 1947. How hard could it be to carry in a few props at the appropriate time with the curtains drawn? I managed to do it, and at times during the many evening rehearsals, even enjoyed it. But, what a difference between the leading man and leading lady (who actually kissed at the end of the play) and me, who was doing my best just to stay hidden in the darkness of the sets backstage. What college would be interested in me with only two extracurricular activities listed after my name?

As it turned out I actually ended up with three. There was little I had to do, or even could do at this point, about the third one. I was nominated to the National Honor Society. My grades were just too high and my teachers gave me their favor, like it or not. Three listings behind my name seemed like a sufficient number. I was done with making the effort to look like an involved student since that's the last thing that I wanted to be in my high school.

Chapter 16

The waves of death swirled about me;
the torrents of destruction overwhelmed me.
The cords of the grave coiled around me;
the snares of death confronted me.
In my distress I called to the Lord;
I called out to my God.
2 Samuel 22:5–7 [NIV]

Where was God in all of this? I really wanted to know. I could not understand how He could let me suffer so horribly and just stand by and watch it happen. I believed in Him and was trying to live my life for Him as much as I had been taught. It was hard to comprehend His care for me while I was suffering so deeply and continuously. In fact, He must have been right there beside me, weeping too. I just didn't know it or sense it at the time.

The reason I can say this now is that, incredibly, I survived those years at all. In my desperation I began to seriously contemplate ending my misery. I was so alone in my pain. If only I could have talked to someone. There was no one that I could trust with my secret, or so it seemed to me at the time. I began to think that the only way to find release from the hurt would be through death.

Prior to that time, I had never given much thought to suicide. I had only heard it mentioned a very few times. One of my brother's friends had committed suicide by shooting himself. His mother, in unspeakable grief, had followed him to her death just a few weeks later. I knew it was a serious and awful thing based on what I overheard my parents saying. Could one even go to heaven after committing suicide? No one seemed to know.

I knew that I could never shoot myself. We did have guns in the house, but they were for hunting or target shooting. I don't think I ever seriously considered ending my pain with a gun.

By that time, in my second year at the new high school, I had my recently acquired driver's license. I was given a fair amount of liberty with one of the family cars. As long as I helped with family errands, I was allowed to use a car when I wanted to go somewhere. That included going back to my old school for ball games, driving to the Christian fellowship meeting at my former principal's house, going out to eat with Lori and Sharon, going shopping for a new shirt or blouse at K-Mart, and even driving to school if I would take my sisters along, too. It was such a relief to not have to ride the school bus. That eliminated at least a portion of the daily discomfort.

When I was alone in the car I began to contemplate what it might be like to end my life while driving a car. Maybe no one would even know it was a suicide. Accidents happened every day. People died every day on the highways. I felt a sense of shame as I toyed with the idea of ending my life. It seemed wrong to even consider it.

In the same way that I had "fixed" my situation to lower my grades and grade point average, I felt I could also permanently fix my largemouth bass situation and the shame and pain that it brought to me daily.

As the suicide fantasy began to grow, it became more detailed over time. I only entertained the thoughts if I was driving alone. When someone else was with me I didn't allow the thoughts to stay.

In my mind's eye I considered a high speed head-on crash with another vehicle, maybe a semi-truck. After watching those purposefully fear-instilling movies in driver's ed. class, I thought that would be a way to effectively end my life and my pain. But, I knew in my heart that I did not want to involve another vehicle. I wasn't out to destroy someone else, just myself. It would be wrong to kill or injure someone else while ending my own pain. I didn't allow that option much run-time in my thoughts. I knew harming someone else was out of the question.

Once I had resolved that possibility I began to look for another plan. It seemed that I needed to drive head-on and full speed into another large object that would stop me cold and dead. On my lone and contemplative drives I finally found the perfect object. It was a large old oak tree at the end of a curve and next to a lightly traveled intersection. No one would have to know that it was a suicide. It was at the top of a slight slope and on a curve. Even the most careful and experienced driver could miss a curve— especially at night. Who could fault a young, inexperienced driver for missing a curve on a dark and rainy night?

In a strange and unhealthy way, that old oak tree became a friend to me. In my death fantasies, it got to the point that I could not approach that oak without contemplating how it could end my self-hate and pain. I would mentally rehearse how I would accelerate to a high speed, aim toward that tree, and just miss the curve. It was on the right side of the road, so I wouldn't need to cross the center line and risk hurting anyone else. Only I would be hurt. I desperately wanted to be done with the embarrassment of being so very ugly and being cruelly reminded of it with no respite.

As I fantasized about my end it would occur to me that maybe something could go wrong. What if I didn't actually die? How seriously would I be hurt? Would I be in trouble for wrecking the family car? What if I lived through it? Then what? Maybe my mouth would look even uglier if I survived a horrible accident!

As I asked earlier, where was God in all of this? Again, I say, I think He was right beside me feeling my pain and grieving with me. He didn't intervene in a humanly visible way, but I do believe that somehow He kept me from carrying out my planned end. He must have had another plan. For some reason, my escape fantasy never became my reality.

To this day, more than forty years later, I think I would be able to pick out that same oak tree on the curve. Undoubtedly, it's older and larger but probably still there on that country road. As I said, that tree became a friend to me. I knew it would be there for me if the desperation became more than I could handle. I knew, if necessary, it could be my escape and release from an unbearable teenaged life.

Chapter 17

As my senior year began, I realized that I only had to survive nine more months of that hell-hole, and I would be free forever, never to return as long as I lived. Being a senior meant the ridicule was less frequent, but it still reared its ugly head often enough to make me unsure of myself in any setting where high school students were present. Actually, any confidence I once may have had, was gone. I couldn't even pretend to have any self-assurance no matter what the situation.

As my senior year progressed I continued to stay away from any of the normal celebrations of youth and high school. Things like homecoming float-building, parades and dances, proms, sporting events, pep rallies, class parties, and group gatherings at nearby pizza joints were things to be avoided, not to be eagerly anticipated. When adults or students quipped that high school should be enjoyed because, "These years are the best years of your life," I was hoping that couldn't possibly be true. My main motivation at that time was escaping those high school years and avoiding further public humiliation.

My crushed confidence and well-practiced evasion techniques carried over to non-school settings, too. I never got involved in my church's youth group to any extent, even though my younger siblings all eventually did. Our church was not in the same town as my new high school, but there were still too many teenagers there for my liking. Who knows if one perceptive teen among them might discover what I really looked like and let it be known to the others? I couldn't chance it, so it was much safer to just not go. I'm surprised that my parents let me get away with that, but maybe they saw that the home fellowship group led by my previous principal was sufficient for my spiritual growth at the time.

During my last three high school years there were only two settings, besides my own home, where I felt safe and unthreatened—that Christian fellowship and 4-H. I lived a self-imposed limited reality, not at all what high school should have been. While my classmates were attempting to live life to the fullest with adventure and fun, I just wanted to stay safely hidden from their view and commentary. I don't know that I ever grieved appropriately for those lost experiences of youth, but undoubtedly it was needed.

My senior year of high school began to wind down toward graduation. By that time I had made the decision to go to college to become a special education teacher. My brother had wonderful teachers that inspired and made me want to be like them. Even with only three high school activities behind my name in the yearbook, it seemed that there were still some colleges that wanted me. I was accepted by all that I applied to, so I only needed to make my decision. Of course, my selection criteria was that the college needed to be big enough so that I could "blend into the woodwork" and not be noticed, and be far enough from my high school that nobody could possibly know my personal history.

As graduation neared, and the seniors eagerly awaited the day when they would walk down the aisle toward adulthood, I became queasy with dread. There was an Honor Society Banquet and a Senior Awards Night to get through. I really had no choice but to go to these events. Even if I could avoid most of the other activities of high school, these were not events to be skipped. In the end, there must have been sufficient parent presence and decorum at these functions, because not one abuse was hurled through the air in my direction. As nervous and scared as I was inside, it was impossible to enjoy these special occasions. They were to be survived, not relished. I couldn't wait for the last benediction to be given, so that I could hurry out the door to the school parking lot, with my parents rushing behind to keep up.

These ordeals were bad enough, but as graduation day loomed I couldn't help thinking of the worst case scenario for my big night. What if, on my last evening of high school, as I walked across the stage to receive my diploma, someone actually had the audacity to yell out "Largemouth Bass"? Or maybe several people would. I knew exactly those who could do it and not feel any remorse for it. I didn't think that, magically, on their last day of school, they would all of a sudden become thoughtful and considerate of another's feelings. I wasn't only concerned about my own classmates, but also about those recently graduated alumni of the last few years who knew me, or the underclassmen in the audience. There was no telling who might be in the audience and be willing to shout out words of humiliation just to get a laugh.

Dear God, how could I walk across that stage all on my own? I knew I had no choice in the matter. It was expected, and graduation was the only way to be done with high school forever. I couldn't really drop out at this point. Believe me, I considered it. While other students were concerned about final exams, senior "skip day", and graduation parties, I was concerned with how to survive the nightmare of the actual graduation event. As my name was called I would have to walk across the stage alone. I couldn't run across the stage for the exit door. I had to walk ceremoniously across and then return to my seat. Only after the formal recessional could I make a break for the car. How was I going to survive this? Those last days were filled with shame, grief, dread, and the realization that I had no choice but to go through with it.

My thoughts were consumed by this and by pleading with God for mercy in the situation. Please, God, just NOT on my graduation night! Hadn't I lived through enough pain and embarrassment? Hadn't I missed out on much of the fun of my high school years? Couldn't I just have this one last night without being "outed" publicly in front of my parents, family, and visiting relatives? In my desperation, I wasn't sure I was going to survive this.

But, on a hot, rainy June evening in 1975, I did survive my graduation night. As I made my way across that lonely awful stage, no one blurted the hurtful words. As I reached my seat with my diploma in hand and my honor cords draped over my shoulders, I almost cried in relief. I had made it across the stage and nobody had hurled any parting shots of pain. Thank you, God for sparing me tonight. It was almost over!

As the ceremony ended, most graduates lingered in and around the gym, hesitant to leave their friends and high school behind. There were smiles, tears, hugs, promises made, and photos taken. Not for me— and the rainy downpour gave me a legitimate reason to run for my car this one last time.

Chapter 18

After surviving my graduation night I thought that I was home free in terms of life, liberty, and the pursuit of happiness. After a summer of horse shows, 4-H, and horses, I would be off to college! I could get on to my real life!

I had decided on a university satellite school three hours from home. This college was known for its high quality special education degree program. Recently passed federal laws were then requiring public schools to provide for their disabled students. Most teacher training colleges were on board with the required program changes, but this university was known to be doing the job exceptionally well. That was fine and good, but I was looking more at whether it was far enough from home to give me a fresh start away from my high school and whether the student population was sufficiently large enough to let me fade into the woodwork. With a student population around 10,000, it seemed that this college would fit my requirements.

It's sort of amazing to me, after having such a horrendous high school experience, that I would want to spend my adult professional career in a school. Being a teacher meant being in a school. Did I really understand that? Even so, I knew that I wanted to be a special education teacher just like the incredible ones that my brother had while he was in school.

Another reason for my career decision was that I wanted to look out for the underdog. I had been one of the underdogs in my high school, and nobody had looked out for me, or so it seemed. Although my brother never attended the same school that I attended, I had seen other special needs high school students mistreated because of their differences. I was deemed different because of my looks; they were deemed different because of their mental ability, or lack thereof. It didn't matter what the perceived differences were, the pain that came along with them was probably the same. It hurt to be ridiculed as an underdog.

I was very excited about college and the chance to start a new life as an adult. Adult life had to be way better than high school life. It just had to be! The people who claimed that your high school years were the best years of your life had to be wrong. I was certain of it!

After a wonderful summer filled with knowing that there'd be no more high school for me, I headed off to college with joy and excitement in my heart. It was a bit hard to leave the safety and security of home, but the adventure ahead seemed worth any feelings of homesickness.

What I found at college was that most people really didn't care who you were or what you looked like. There were people of all shapes, sizes, colors, abilities, oddities, and personalities. I actually felt like I could, indeed, blend into the woodwork. I didn't need to stand out as exceptional in the awful way that I had in high school.

I had chosen not to live in the well-known party dorms, and in fact, lived in a dorm with a fourth floor academic quiet hall where the "boring" bookish students chose to live. That might have contributed to the protection of my self-esteem. Most of the other students on my floor were committed to attending college to actually get an education and not just have a wild, drunken party experience away from the limits set down by their moms and dads.

That is not to say that nobody ever partied on my floor or made a derogatory remark to me about my looks, because there were a few who did. Even after

35 years I can still remember a gal from my floor, who was inebriated quite often. How she ended up living on the quiet floor I do not know. I'm guessing her college decision came late, like in early September, and a room on the academic floor may have been one of the few still available. She certainly had no commitment to anything besides having a good time, or so it appeared to me. As I recall, she didn't even last out the year.

When she was drinking, which she did frequently, she liked to sing. When she saw me, she would launch into a song from a TV commercial that advertised *Chicken of the Sea* brand tuna fish. Coincidental? Not likely! Obviously, the fish theme continued, but at least it wasn't quite as blatant as the largemouth bass torment of high school. When this girl left, or flunked out, there were no tears of sadness from me. I was happy to see her go.

With her degrading song for me, she was the exception and not the rule. In general, most other students just went about their daily lives minding their own business. College was very different than high school. Thank God for that!

Although the intentional cruelty of high school was behind me, unfortunately the damage to my psyche was not. The damage done in those three years of high school would impact me for the rest of my life in one way or another. I did not realize it at the time, but the emotional baggage I was carrying would be lugged around for many, many years to come.

Chapter 19

What I did not realize then, or for those many, many years to come, was how very deeply I was scarred in my heart and emotions. I thought since high school was behind me, along with the ridicule and torment, I would be fine. College seemed to be different in the fact that most other people went about their business with not a lot of thought about me or my looks. I was "blending into the woodwork" of a larger school population, just as I had hoped.

Yet, there was a sadness and brokenness within me that I couldn't seem to comprehend or even put into words. Determinedly, I purposely did not put any of it into words. As I had kept my secret in high school, so I held it even more closely now. The last thing I wanted to do was talk about or tell anyone of my high school experiences in this new locale.

Even when I made new friends, who probably could have related to what I had experienced, I never spoke the words. Many of my new friends lived on my same quiet, academic, dormitory floor and were obviously there for the purpose of getting an education. Most of them appeared to be underdogs in their own way. Even the beautiful girl across the hall seemed to have a dark secret that kept her shut off from reaching her potential as a social butterfly. Candidly, most of my new friends were social misfits in one way or another. Maybe that is what drew us together as friends. Even so, they did not need to know my past. I allowed the dark secrets to grip my soul ever more tenaciously.

In many ways I felt happier than I had for a very long time. But the feelings of happiness, security, and safety were only skin deep. Any happiness that I felt was fragile and shallow. I felt always on guard and ready for the next hurtful words to come. Deeper inside was an unsettled turmoil that I tried to ignore.

To that point, my positive experiences with males (other than my dad and brothers) had been very limited. At times I had taken notice of and been interested in guys at 4-H meetings and activities, at horse shows, at the Christian fellowship group, and while playing or watching basketball with my brother and his friends. None of those situations could have been remotely considered a date.

In my senior year of high school, I had spent some time with a guy who actually had the courage to say hello to me in the hall one day. He, too, was a social misfit who probably felt he had nothing to lose by saying hello to the Largemouth Bass. We spent some time together at his family's dairy farm, went to a concert together, and snowmobiled together. I suppose those times could have loosely been called dates. When I left for college he gave me a begonia plant for my dorm room and even wrote to me several times during my freshman year.

In hindsight, I realize what a wonderful guy he must have been to be willing to risk being fully ostracized by acknowledging me as a friend. Unfortunately, with my feelings of self-loathing and ugliness, I couldn't wholly appreciate his friendship. In school and in town, I avoided being seen with him because I thought it would draw attention to me. I was trying not to be seen or be noticed. Although he was always kind to me, our being together would have been something for my tormentors to take note of, and I surely didn't want that! I was so determined to avoid pain and humiliation that I was not very considerate of what he might have been feeling. We never officially broke up because we had never officially been dating. Besides, I was leaving for an out-of-town college!

Very early in my freshman year of college, I ran into an old friend from my childhood—in other words, from my "old" school. Unbeknownst to me, he had decided to attend this same college for their successful baseball program. He had been a pitcher in high school and had hoped to play in college. He was away from home for the first time and much more homesick than me. He was definitely a "mama's boy" and was looking for a substitute while he had to be away from home. I believed myself to be ugly and couldn't consider that a guy, any guy, would actually show some interest in me. Somehow we started having our meals together and became boyfriend and girlfriend. Apart from a lot of shared and immature laughter, it was not an emotionally healthy boy-girl relationship. Although it took until Christmas, he was the first guy to ever kiss me. He really didn't kiss me often, which was probably a good thing. When our classes ended in May and he went home to be with his mom, our relationship ended. The good thing about this, my first real dating relationship, was that it was quite innocent and helped both of us get through our first year away from home.

As unhealthy as this relationship was, it was also a bit surprising to me. Here was actually a nice-looking, athletic guy that seemed to like me! My self-esteem was so low in the gutter that I could hardly fathom that he or anyone else could like me. It came as a shock to me! Being a part of a "couple" with him made me feel like I had some value. That lasted until mid-May when he went home to be with his mother. I struggled with the realization that I had been used by him to offset his homesickness. It made me mad, but at least I hadn't gotten too physically involved with him. I thought that was probably a good thing. The couple thing was over, and I felt ugly once more.

Chapter 20

Although my first few relationships with boys were quite innocent, it wasn't too long before my low self-esteem, the freedom of college, and the sexually-liberated culture of the times came crashing together to make a foul mess. I should have known better, and in fact, I did know better, based on what the Bible said to me. But, other than my own reading of the Bible, no adults were giving me any encouragement to keep my way pure. Once I left for college I didn't involve myself in any youth ministries or campus fellowship groups. I walked to church a mile or two from campus on the weekends that I didn't go home, but I only slipped in and out quickly for the Sunday morning services. Knowing better and doing better were two very different things.

My parents assumed their children would walk in purity, and never really discussed it with us, or at least with me. Even if they had, I'm quite sure it would have just been a mandate to do so, without any "how-to" attached to it. I really was adrift and alone when it came to the topic of sexual purity.

In this current age, people talk about purity pledges and secondary virginity if you've made past bad choices. Girls sometimes get purity rings from their parents before they start down the dating road. There are public conversations on the ramifications of dating vs. courtship. There are countless books on the topic of sexual purity for young adults. Most Christian youth groups discuss it honestly and often.

In the 1970s and early '80s, when I was a young adult, there was no such talk. If you messed up, you were messed up for life. If you lost your way, purity-wise, there was no going back and no second chances. There was nothing to maintain or recoup once the line had been crossed. Although I had good, reasonably moral friends and roommates in college, there was nobody cheering me on to make right and pure choices.

After feeling so humiliated and ugly through my high school years, it felt wonderful to have guys take notice of me and actually want to date me. It gave me some perceived value in my own eyes. I couldn't really believe that I had any value of my own. It was dating a guy that gave me value. When guys gave me attention, it made me feel like I wasn't so ugly after all, at least for a short time.

However, giving yourself away a little tiny piece at a time does nothing to build your self-esteem. Regret, guilt, and shame are not exactly esteem-builders for someone who knows better in her heart. Yet, I seemed unable to make godlier and healthier choices. With every line that was crossed, there was no going back, nothing to recover, and no chance to start over. The feelings of ugliness were now no longer about my physical appearance but in my heart of sin, too. It wasn't that I had a multitude of partners; I did not. But, living your life outside of God's plan always causes damage.

Consider too, purity isn't just avoiding sexual intercourse in your dating relationships. It is purity of the heart before God. There are many small acts of impurity that lead you down a path of no return, or should I say, seemingly, a path of no return. With each sinful choice, it seems that much more difficult to back away from the precipice. When you believe that you have no value apart from the guy you are with, it is easy to be swept into wrong choices. Even if you know that it is not what God would want for you, as I did know in my heart of hearts. God was somewhere afar off; this guy holding me was easier to hear. When you feel like a worthless, ugly, largemouth bass, there seems no reason not to self-destruct. The cliff was there...why not jump?

Chapter 21

To this point, I haven't really said much about satan, called the father of lies in John 8:44. [For the full scripture, please see the Appendix.] But, now is the time to start. (I will always use a lower-case s on his name. I refuse to capitalize it no matter what my high school English teacher might say.) I now believe that what happened to me in high school was not specifically in God's will for me, but He allowed it to happen. God was there all the time, and I do believe that He was grieved for what was happening to me, but for whatever His purposes, He allowed it to happen. I believe that he bottled my tears, the ones cried and the many uncried, to hold for eternity. He could have stopped the bullying, or even prevented it from ever happening at all. But, He did not. Not even when I daily begged for His mercy to make it end.

As I mentioned early on in my story, I truly did have my own and very personal spiritual awakening while in junior high and before the big move to our new town. While attending the Sunday night fellowship at my principal's house, I experienced God in all three forms: Father, Jesus, and Holy Spirit. I went to church with my family and worshipped with them, but it became personal for me when I went to the fellowship group.

At that same time I also attended a David Wilkerson Crusade in Madison, Wisconsin. David Wilkerson, author of the book *The Cross and the Switchblade* (1962), had a compassionate heart for young people. It was there that I committed my young life to Christ and to being a "Jesus Freak" for real. I carried my Bible to school and wasn't afraid to share my faith. That wonderful boldness and sense of being on fire for Christ guided each of my days. That is not to say that I lived my life perfectly and without sin; after all I was a real, living, breathing teenager! But, my greatest desire was to please my Savior and Friend, Jesus.

I think the reality of my vibrant commitment to Christ was connected in two ways to the spiritual realm. I believe that God knew that in order for me to survive (literally!) what was ahead, I would need to have his Spirit to help me through. Although I often felt abandoned by God during those ensuing years, I now know that it was He who somehow kept me from suicide when there seemed to be no other way.

Somehow He helped me to survive what felt like the impossible and unbearable.

On the opposite end of the spiritual spectrum was satan, the deceiver. I am positive that he was not happy about my joy in the Lord and willingness to share it with anyone ready to listen. High school is a prime opportunity for satan to draw young ungrounded people into his traps (drugs, alcohol, sex, pornography, faithlessness, etc.) that can bind them for a lifetime. Undoubtedly, he was not happy to have me standing in the gap to prevent that from happening, at least with some of those in my small sphere of influence. I'm guessing (in my very limited, but well-thought-through human viewpoint) that satan did not want me taking my joy and God's word into my new school setting where there was no fellowship group up to that point in time.

Starting on Day 1 of my new school experience, he was ready for the battle, with all of his demons at his beck and call. I was armed, but apparently not ready spiritually, for the onslaught that he leveled against me. My boldness for Jesus Christ was pretty much shot to hell in a matter of a few days. My only goal became hiding both me and "this little light of mine." Even when I cried out to God to make it stop, there seemed to be no answer. I was in the situation alone with no one to rescue me. Or at least that is how it seemed to me.

The battle raged against and around me. I was so caught off-guard by the onslaught that it seemed I was defenseless. I didn't know how to fight the battle. I didn't know much about the tricks of our enemy, satan. I did not know that from the time I was born he was working on a plan to steal, kill, and destroy me (John 10:10). His plan was coming to fruition, or so it seemed. I'm sure he was glee-filled as he saw me emotionally cowering and broken-hearted just weeks into my new life situation and high school. There were no words of witness for Christ from my lips. I was trying to hide, not light a candle for all to see. I became powerless for Christ in a very short amount of time. I was down for the count. The battle was lost. It seemed that satan had won, and the defeat would last for decades to come.

This powerlessness was the story of my life through the college years and into my early professional life. Fear, insecurity, and low self-esteem controlled me.

Chapter 22

No longer was I much of a witness for my Lord. In the years after high school I became bound by my own craving to just fit in, which led to many poor choices. I was walking an inconsistent life that left me nothing to witness about. I was as bound in my sin as the average non-Christian walking out their young adult life. I still would have claimed to be a Christian, but the fruit of my life was hypocrisy. I could still talk the Jesus-talk when I needed to, but I certainly wasn't walking the Jesus-walk with any consistency. I was living a life of lies.

I was trying to straddle this very tricky fence between living the life of a Christian and a life in the world without Christ. I lived with one leg on each side of the fence. It was an uncomfortable place to be! I was a lousy Christian and a lousy sinner. I couldn't walk on either side of the fence very well. I knew too much about the other side to be very successful on either side.

My college years went by quickly. I finished college in just three and a half years and was fortunate to find a teaching position mid-year. I was hired before Thanksgiving, but I needed to officially graduate in December and then finish out my student teaching experience. How utterly exciting and overwhelming to be a freshly-graduated special education teacher with a new job in a small, rural school district! I finished my student teaching on a Friday, moved on the weekend, and started teaching on a Monday in late January. It was a thrilling but very scary time of life. Looking back, I'm not sure how I managed it. God must have been holding my hand and guiding me, in spite of the hypocrite's life that I was living. He saw promise and victory ahead, where I saw none.

Being in a new job, in a new town, with new people to meet, I lived my life trying to prove I was just like everyone else. I wanted to fit in, no matter what that meant. I did not want to stand out as different in any way that would draw attention to me. I continued to compromise, making bad choices as they came along, if only it meant not standing out as unusual or different. I became controlled by my fear of rejection.

In this new small town environment, there were occasionally people who took notice of my looks and made comments relative to my fishy lips. Some of them were grown men who had never matured beyond junior high. One teacher, in particular, thought he was very funny when he used puns in his conversations, doing it with nauseating reliability. This was his means to get a few laughs, and he used them every chance that he could. Of course, he had a heyday at my expense! The twisted part of it was that I believe he thought that I didn't know what he was doing. It's hard to imagine what kind of a person does that purposefully, to entertain himself or others in the room, at another's expense. This was a man who was a teacher of junior high students, who are commonly struggling with their own self-esteem. It's interesting to me that his maturity level never advanced much beyond that of his students. He frequently used puns in the classroom with his students. It is likely that bullying was not only committed by the students in his classroom but by the supposed professional, too!

On occasion there were others who made cracks or used word play to make it known how they saw me. It further emphasized to me that I was ugly, no two ways about it! Even if nobody had ever actually said any "fish" words aloud, I still knew what I had been told and believed the lie. There seemed to be no way of escaping it. I believed in my heart that is how everyone saw me, whether they actually commented or not. I had the notion that even my friends saw me that way, only they were just too nice to say it.

I could be anywhere...out alone, or with friends. If I overheard anyone talking about anything relative to the sport of fishing, a Friday night fish-fry, a Door County fish boil, a recipe they cooked for dinner last night, or anything even remotely related to the word fish, I cringed inside. My anxiety level increased wildly and I could feel it in every cell of my body. It hit me hardest in the gut. It would take hours, if not days, to talk myself down from the grief and distress. I believed that somehow the talk was about me. Most of the time the overheard conversation probably had nothing to do with me, but I perceived that my lips were the biggest thing in the room and would always be. My saddened heart and downturned frown only magnified the look. The cruelty of the past had become the reality of my present and seemingly would be my future, too.

It seemed that I would never escape my largemouth bass persona. It was here to stay! I hated myself and how I looked.

Chapter 23

During those early years as a young teaching professional, I lived in emotional turmoil most of the time. Living in a small town in the middle of nowhere, I felt bored and lonely (although I did make some truly good friends that have remained my life-long friends). I found myself struggling to fit in, to be accepted, and to be acceptable. Fear of rejection seemed to be my constant companion.

I'm going to guess that learning to be an adult is probably difficult for most people—it certainly was for me. In spite of being smart, efficient, organized, goal-oriented, professional, and independent, I found myself floundering. I was so trapped by insecurity and self-esteem that was lower-than-low, that I just couldn't feel much sense of joy or success in anything. I pretty much felt like a loser all the time. It didn't matter if it was about my verbal contribution to a professional team meeting or my dish for a potluck; I felt like a failure. A broken dating relationship, followed by some more bad choices, did nothing to make me feel better about myself. The self-hatred from deep within made me feel hopeless for any kind of a better life.

At one point in those first few years of teaching, two of my sisters began to feel concerned about me. It was nearing Christmas, and they sensed that I was really struggling emotionally. Although they knew that I would be coming home for the holidays soon, they decided to drive the three hours to come and see, in person, how I was doing.

What they probably didn't realize at that time was that I was becoming severely depressed. After much prodding as to what was troubling me, I began for the very first time to tell them about what had happened to me in high school. My oldest sister had been living in Seattle, thousands of miles away, during my high school years and had no clue about any of it. My other sister was the next younger after me, but she claimed she didn't know about what had happened. She was two years behind me and attended the middle school during my first torturous year at the new high school. By the time she was a freshman at my same school, I was a junior. Our school building somewhat segregated the under- and upperclassmen. She denied knowing anything about my being bullied.

I only revealed a little of the truth, but they could tell by my deep grieving sobs that it had been bad for me. It brought me some immediate relief to have told someone who cared about me, even if it was just a little piece of what had happened. I felt emotionally able to continue on for a few more weeks until the Christmas break when I could go home and be with my family.

While I was home for Christmas, I was shocked and very angered to find out that my oldest sister had revealed my deeply-held and tightly-guarded secret to my parents. I don't know that I ever made her promise not to, but how could she break a confidence? I felt so embarrassed about it, yet that was the last emotion that I should have felt. I had done nothing wrong to deserve what had happened to me.

My parents repeatedly said how sorry they were that it had happened, that they hadn't known about it at the time, and that they had done nothing to rescue me. (How could they have known?) They felt terrible about it all. And I didn't feel any too happy that they now knew. Even so, I do think it gave me some relief that they finally knew a hint of some of the pain I had endured. Besides being sorry, my dad tried to share situations from his boyhood where he had been bullied and how he had bounced back to have a good life in spite of it. He felt it was nothing a positive attitude couldn't ultimately fix.

My mom's solution was to tell me that I was a very pretty girl and that I didn't need to believe any of it. OK, well that sounded like a good quick fix to my pain! Unfortunately the years of being told otherwise and believing it in your heart and soul had a bit more power over me than my mom's simple solution. I know her heart was right, and she was just trying to make me feel better, but it just wasn't going to be enough.

As much as I didn't want them to know about any of it, I think it did bring a small sense of relief deep inside of me. It was no longer quite as heavy a burden to bear. Not that I was going to bring the subject up again with my parents, but at least they knew something of what had happened to me. As far as I was concerned we wouldn't be talking about it again.

After the holidays I returned to my apartment, seemingly at the end of the planet, and set about to live my life as an adult. The struggle for any sense of a positive self-esteem continued. I did the best I could, with what I had, as I fumbled along trying to find myself.

Chapter 24

As a young adult living on my own, I continued to try to find my way personally and as a professional. I tried to be happy, but I never really felt that way for long or with any authenticity. I was damaged on the inside, and there seemed no real way to heal that, even knowing what I knew about God from the Bible. Shouldn't God be able to heal these heart wounds? I wanted Him to heal me once and for all. It didn't seem like He was able. I kept thinking that He should be able to do this, but the healing never came no matter how much I prayed, pleaded, or begged.

Based on her bumper sticker, I took note that one of my new friends and coworkers at school had gone to a Christian university, so I assumed that she was a Christian. Her parents certainly seemed to be when I had occasional contact with them. They invited me to various Christian functions, and I eventually started going to church with my friend on a regular basis in a nearby town. We never really talked about our faith in a personal way but just made assumptions about each other as the friendship developed. Many times I would feel encouraged or hopeful after a sermon, but it would be short-lived and I would again struggle with my self-esteem. We would attend annual women's conferences together, and I would buy a book or two that seemed to totally relate to my need for emotional healing or dealing with self-esteem issues. I faithfully read the books, but nothing really seemed to change or ease my pain for more than a short time. I felt without hope of ever feeling differently than I did then. Something would come along; a comment, a word, real or imagined, directed at me or not, that made me again feel like nothing but an ugly looking fish-faced largemouth bass. I just could not get out from under the pain I was living with every single day.

These feelings of worthlessness and ugliness impacted every area of my life. Although I was a successful young school teacher, who was well thought of and respected in my school and community, I could see nothing but ugliness. When people would compliment me for anything, I would usually respond with a "Well, but....," kind of reply. I was even told by my immediate professional supervisor that, "The correct response is thank you," on many occasions. It was hard for me to believe anything good could come from me. In spite of all of my many strengths, particularly academic and professional strengths, I could only see and feel failure. If anyone had something nice to say of me, I believed that it was not to be believed. I feared that soon someone would point out the real me and they would see the ugliness, too.

Chapter 25

During those early teaching years as I was desperately trying to find something to like about myself, I met a young man named Mike. He was a local guy who was younger than I was by four years, but old enough to drink alcohol and shake dice at a local establishment. Our town was small and rural with very few choices for places that young people could meet. While my parents would have definitely preferred that I look for a young man at church, meeting a guy there seemed highly unlikely to me. I believed that finding a boyfriend would raise my value and allow me to like myself. I thought a young man could heal my wounds once and for all, so I was desperate to find any guy who could like me.

At that time and place in my life, I enjoyed one particular local bar because it had a lighted dance floor. After all, this was the decade of disco! I enjoyed dancing with my girlfriends or even alone. That night I had come into the bar in the company of another local young man. We were not in any way romantically involved with each other; we were just passing time on a Saturday night. He and I had spent time together on a few occasions, but he actually was engaged to a girl living in different state. Mike was shaking dice with a mutual friend and that is how we met. I liked him right away because he did not in any way give a hint that he thought of me as ugly. He was just being a guy. When he won the dice shake, he was a gentleman and shared his prizes with me, which of course were alcoholic drinks.

I have to say that even though I was an emotional mess inside, I was smart enough when it came to alcohol. My parents had taught me well! They were teetotalers, and I had never once seen them drink in my lifetime. They had warned me about the dangers of alcohol while I was growing up. I appreciated their serious training on the subject, but more than anything, I did not like the feeling of losing control. I am happy to say that I have never once been drunk in my life. There have been times I felt a bit tipsy or silly, but I never allowed myself to reach the point of drunkenness. This was undoubtedly a good thing since I liked to go to dance bars and at the same time was looking for a guy to like me. Alcohol could have tipped the scales to disastrous and dangerous outcomes.

During the course of this July evening, the guy who brought me into the bar said he was going to leave, to which I responded that I was going to stay. I told him I would find my own way home. My apartment was less than a mile away, but I was hoping this new attraction named Mike would give me a ride home. I asked him and he agreed to it. Mike continued to shake dice, drink a few, and finally got up the courage to ask this young school teacher to dance. Of course, I was thrilled! He must not have thought of me as ugly or he wouldn't have asked me to dance. That was my thinking. What did I know about young men? Maybe he would be the boyfriend who made me feel good about myself!

He did drive me home that night, walked me to my door, and gave me a kiss goodnight. I was thrilled and excited to see where this might lead. The following weekend, while walking to the baseball diamond with my single teacher girlfriends, I saw Mike headed into the disco bar. I decided to join him instead and left my girlfriends behind!

At the time that Mike and I met, it was summer vacation and I was actually looking to leave this out-in-the-boondocks small town to move closer to my family and back to the city. I was enjoying my summer vacation, had actually resigned my teaching position, and was setting up interviews in larger towns closer to my family home. Special education was a new field in the 1970s, and the recent federal mandate made many new jobs for a limited number of licensed teachers. I was not in any way worried about finding a job and was quite lackadaisical about it all. I was confident that I would get a new teaching job soon.

After Mike and I met he warned me not to stay in town for him, that he was not that serious about me. I concurred that we were not that serious, so I certainly would not stay for him. What else could I say?

As it turned out, many quick changes happened within the local school district where I had been working. There was an administrative change, the teacher that had been hired to take my place took a different job elsewhere, and my position reopened. On an August morning after a Board of Education meeting, I got a call saying my position was open again and would I like to come back and teach for another year? Meeting Mike had changed how I felt about leaving this rinky-dink town, and I decided to stay. It was the easiest path to take! I could end my job search, not worry about moving to a new town and apartment, and possibly find love with Mike. I felt happy about life because I had a boyfriend. Because of him, I could like myself just a little and try to convince myself that I was pretty, after all!

Chapter 26

Mike and I enjoyed the rest of the summer together before I returned to school in the fall. It was wonderful to start the new school year with a boyfriend. Having Mike in my life helped me consider, and try to persuade myself, that the kids in high school had possibly all been wrong. Who were they to tell me that I was ugly? Mike apparently didn't think that I was, or at least he was willing to be seen in public with me. I certainly never asked him what he thought of my looks, at least not in the early months of our budding relationship.

Truthfully, even then as a young adult, and much more so now, when I consider some of my tormentors, I can't imagine why I let them bully me without fighting back, or at least saying something to them. Many of them had their own issues that could have been candidly pointed out. Some had serious acne issues and scars, and some were quite overweight. (It could be argued that they were not really overweight since they were players on the football team.) Some were poor students academically. Many were from messed up and divorced family homes. I had beautiful skin, was lean and trim, was very bright, and came from a loving Christian home.

Shouldn't I have had some sense of worth to stand on? No, that had been easily and steadily tormented out of me, and as hard as I tried to convince myself otherwise, I could not persuade myself of anything other than what I had been told by the high school bullies.

As a young adult, I would repeatedly ask myself such questions as, "Who were they to say I was ugly or looked like a fish? What made them right? Who were they to talk about me when they had all those acne scars or were fat?" Although I could logically ask these questions, and I seemed to have reasonable answers that would say they had no right to do what they had done, I still couldn't make myself feel any better. There was no way for me to logically explain myself out of what had happened. Even if I could be logical and rational about it, it didn't seem to matter now. What had happened to me in the hallways and classrooms had been real and painful. No amount of logic could erase it or make it go away. My brain logic was not lining up with the feelings of my heart and mind, so I believed my damaged emotions instead of the logic.

Chapter 27

Those first months of getting to know Mike and feeling like his special girl were delightful! He was working the p.m. shift at a factory in the area. I spent part of my lunch break at school calling his home to chat before he headed off to work. (This was tough to do because at that time, our school had only two phones that could be used by the teaching staff.) He would awaken me each weeknight with a phone call around 11:00 p.m. when he got off his work shift. I didn't mind the lost sleep! I was young and a phone call from him was worth every moment! We would both live for the weekends when we could actually be together in person.

When Mike and I went on dates out in public, I had a sense of confidence and at least felt a little bit pretty. He wasn't big on giving me compliments, but the rare one kept me going for at least a little while. Even while I was with him, I was always on alert for some "fishy" innuendo that he might make, and especially any comments that might be made by others in a public setting. I was holding a dark secret that I did not want him to know about. I was always concerned about hiding the truth of what I believed about myself, and lived in fear that he might eventually think the same of me.

If grown men at another table were talking about a weekend fishing trip, a good bait to use for Northern pike, or even about ordering the Friday night perch plate off the menu that night, my mind went to FISH and me. I was certain that they had spotted me across the room and were joking or talking about me. It was usually men's comments that I feared and distrusted the most, based on the fact that most of my tormentors had been male. I was wary of women, too, if I thought they might be commenting on my looks.

No amount of trying to mentally persuade myself otherwise could help me. My immediate reaction was to become quiet, hide inside myself, and take on the sad countenance of what was in my heart. I'm sure it was horribly confusing to Mike to have me change from his bubbly, chatty, happy-to-see-him date to a very quiet, sullen, sad-faced girl right before his eyes with no inkling of why or what had happened. He had no idea of what was racing through my mind! He likely thought that he had somehow offended me and didn't know how. He would ask me what was the matter and, of course, I could only reply, "Nothing." We might be having a great time together and all of a sudden the balloon would burst. I wanted to hurry through dinner and get out and away from whatever was causing me to hurt. I'm sure my eyes were racing and darting wildly in their sockets right along with my mind. When faced with "fight or flight" I wanted to flee, and the sooner the better!

Even after departing the restaurant or other setting, I remained quiet and likely wasn't a lot of fun. I attempted to act "normal" for Mike, but in truth, situations like these would take me days to work through psychologically. With or without Mike present, I was trying to mentally and emotionally digest what had happened and convince myself that what I had overheard had absolutely nothing to do with me or my looks. It was a grim task and I rarely succeeded. I frequently prayed to God for His comfort and help, but He seemed insufficient for my need. I could not seem to access the comfort that I was so needing and desiring.

Chapter 28

Somehow even with all of these ugly undercurrents that I could not explain to Mike, we enjoyed each other's company enough to stay together as a dating couple. Although I loved being his girlfriend, I always carried with me this fear that he might someday see me in a different light. I thought that eventually he would see the real me or that someone would point it out to him. I think there were times when people made comments to him about "taking up fishing" or "reeling her in", but he somehow missed the painful innuendo that sent me ducking for cover for days afterward—emotional cover!

In any case, he was the first of us to voice the words, "I love you." I retorted smartly that no, he was too young to possibly know this. I'm sure that I was thrilled to hear this sentiment from him, but I also doubted that it could be true. Who could really love me if they knew the truth about me? He obviously didn't know or see my truth.

Mike persisted with the idea of love and certainly made me feel loved and special. In due course he got up the courage to ask me to marry him. I responded that I needed to think about it, but OK, yes, I would marry him. I'm sure that he was a little disappointed by my uncertainty and less than enthusiastic reply!

At that point, it became abundantly clear to me that I needed to tell Mike the truth about my hurtful past and then see if he still wanted to marry me. I REALLY DID NOT WANT TO TELL HIM! But, I thought that if there was to be any way that we were going to be married and end up together, I needed to be straight with him on what had happened, see if he agreed with my tormentors once he knew about it, and let him know the significance and toll this had taken on my everyday life.

On my chronological timeline I was about five years beyond high school graduation, but the pain of those days was ever with me. I think I was convinced it would always be, but I was also hopeful for some miraculous healing that would make it go away. Maybe marriage was the miracle that I was looking for? But, before that, I knew I needed to give Mike the opt-out by telling him the truth. That was the only fair thing to do. I decided that in the end, telling him myself might be less embarrassing than having someone else tell him. I felt sick with what I knew had to be done.

I struggled for courage and practiced in my head how I might tell him. Being the goal-oriented person I was, I made my decision firmly and looked for my chance. When the day and time seemed right, it was all I could do to literally spit out those first horrible words. I was almost physically ill by the time I actually jumped in with my story of misery and self-hate. Mike didn't seem particularly shocked by what I was telling him. He gave the impression of studying my face, and especially my mouth, trying to figure out exactly what it was that I wanted him to know. While I was desperately and carefully choosing my words, Mike held me close, and didn't seem to show the revulsion that I was expecting. I did not sense any less love coming from him. He just seemed to be deep in thought while I talked.

After struggling through my story Mike told me that he also had been the victim of bullying, but in junior high, and by his supposed and longtime friends. He said he felt desperate and rejected at the time and had thoughts of suicide, too. His rescue came when his parents made the financial decision to move to a new town. It gave him a fresh start where he was well received as the handsome, strong, broad-shouldered, partying newcomer to the school. His new school had been his rescue!! I was shocked by his similar sad story but also dumb-founded that his new school had been his rescue! How could that have been? He did not seem to have any lingering pain that he carried along with him in his daily life. He didn't live in fear that someone would find out and repeat his story aloud. Or none that he would admit. The main thing that he still didn't seem to understand was why his longtime friends had suddenly turned on him. He had grown up with them as friends and then somehow became the neighborhood outcast. He really didn't know why that had happened, but he also didn't seem to be dragging the pain along with him each day like I was doing.

After hearing his similar, although in my mind, much less painful story, I experienced confusion and disbelief. I knew Mike quite well by this time and I found him to be handsome and smart and I could see little in him that could be picked out for bullying. I felt confused about why he had been a target for meanness. He certainly seemed confused about the "why" of it as well.

As we talked over our mutual painful experiences as victims of bullies, I felt the need to lay it on the line with Mike. I was very direct in telling him that if he EVER used this information against me in any way that we would be done and over for good....married or not. I made sure that he knew in no uncertain terms that he could never use these vicious names or even insinuations against me. All he could say was that he never would do that. That was what I needed to hear from him.

From my viewpoint, Mike now knew the worst about me and seemed not to love me any less. That scary day of revealing my worst hurts and fears became the defining day of my love for Mike. From that day forward we moved quickly toward our wedding day and all the joy that married life would bring!

Chapter 29

The early weeks and months of marriage were happy and full of all the adjustments that most couples must make. Mike moved into the apartment where I had been living, we both continued in our same jobs, and we learned how to live as a married couple. I think we adjusted about as well as any of my other friends who were getting married around the same time. I cannot remember any major difficulties as we learned how to be married. Marriage was mostly good!

But what should come rearing its ugly head? My damaged emotions concerning how I looked and how I thought others saw me! Marriage was not the miracle healer that I was hoping it would be. Our marriage was good but something ugly continued to "swim" below the surface. It was always there but not because of anything that Mike ever said or implied. He was supportive whenever I told him I was feeling ugly and what had triggered the hated feelings. Even though he was reassuring he couldn't seem to fix things for me. Nothing he could say really brought me the peace that I was lacking. I wanted him to fix me and make everything better, but he simply could not do it.

Early in our marriage our local dentist told me that he was taking some orthodontic classes and could make me some dental appliances or even put metal braces on my teeth. His office was right across the street from our apartment and it would be so convenient for me. Putting braces on me would give him the needed orthodontic practice and straighten my teeth in the process. I listened intently to what he had to say. He was not promising anything other than to practice what he was learning in his classes.

What I was hearing was something entirely different. I was hearing that maybe, just maybe, braces would help change the shape of my mouth. Potentially, I could be through with looking like a largemouth bass once and for all. Maybe he would provide the miracle cure for all of my problems. I set about to persuade Mike that this was really important to me and that I wanted to get braces now as an adult. He did not see the need for braces and felt it would be a big waste of money. I pressured, pleaded, and begged and finally Mike gave in to my wishes. He really wanted me to be happy, and if this was the one thing that would do it, then let's go ahead with the braces.

Braces meant a lot of money paid out, tooth and gum discomfort, and a Waterpik on the bathroom counter. It meant no gum chewing and sometimes painful and awkward kissing. I was willing to put up with all of the inconveniences of adult braces if only for a wild potential chance at looking better and finally feeling good about myself. Mike was less excited with the inconveniences, but if it would finally make his wife truly happy, then OK, he would make the needed sacrifices, too.

During the process of tooth straightening it became clear that there wasn't going to be any real change in the shape of my mouth. My teeth might end up a little straighter and it was definitely easier to bite through a sandwich or burger, but there was no substantive change in my overall appearance. I was disappointed, but I didn't dare tell Mike how I was feeling as the braces came off. I was happy with my straighter teeth and the ability to bite clean through a sandwich, but the big change that I was wildly hoping for never materialized. There went a lot of money down the drain! I still looked like a largemouth bass in my mind and emotions. The braces had done nothing to change that, and I still felt ugly on the inside and the outside.

Chapter 30

Unbelievably, and as unlikely as this may seem, one of my younger sisters actually married a young man that had bullied me in school. I was already away from home and attending college by the time they began dating. He was about five years older than my sister, and two years older than me. He was part of the intense bullying that had happened in my first year at the new school, but with him as a graduating senior, for that one year only. My sister did not know yet about my trauma in high school and certainly did not know that her fiancé played a part in it. In fact, neither did I know, specifically. I knew that many people, mostly guys, had caused me great pain, but I went so deep inside of myself at the time that I cannot necessarily remember every face of torment, especially those of the upperclassmen. I thought that maybe his brother had played a part in it, but I was unsure. For the guys in my actual grade I can remember every individual clearly because I was antagonized by them for three full years.

I was excited to be one of my sister's bridesmaids and wanted her to be wonderfully happy. Her husband seemed to be a godly man and certainly was very helpful and caring toward my parents and to my disabled brother. I was extremely nervous on her wedding day as I was coupled with the groom's brother, who I specifically did remember from school. I did what I needed to do as her bridesmaid on her beautiful day, and thankfully everyone was on their best behavior.

Beyond their wedding day I wasn't around him much, except for holidays and family gatherings, so I did not live with any specific avoidance of him. My only apprehension of him was that I knew that he was aware of what had happened to me in school, and I did not want him talking to my sister or any family members about it. I was hoping that the subject would not come up between them. When they married I was still very much in the secret-keeping phase of my pain!

Later, after Mike and I married, we ended up staying in their home whenever we were in the area overnight. I was very close to my sister, and Mike thought of her husband as his brother-in-law and friend. Our relationship grew and nothing was ever said about our former high school days. I am unsure of how much he actually told my sister, but a few years into our marriage my brother-in-law asked if he could speak to me privately.

My first thought was, "Oh, no! Here it comes!" I wasn't ready to face anything that he had to say, but it felt like I had no choice at the time. At best, it was an awkward and difficult conversation. Both of us struggled with what to say. He told me that he was very sorry for what he had done to me in school. He admitted that he was one of my tormentors at least on a few occasions. He explained that as a shorter-than-average boy in school he had been picked on, too. He said that he should have never joined in, but he had, and he was sorry. All I could say at the time was, "OK". I did not give much of a response, and the conversation did not go very far because I was not ready or able to talk of it with him or anyone else at that time in my life. My sister later said that her husband really was sorry for what he had done to me. Again my response was a simple, "OK". I could say no more. I did not ask her what she knew of what had happened because I really did not want to know or even talk about it with her. She likely would have provided me some comfort if I had only let her in to my broken places.

Chapter 31

The struggle continued as I longed to accept and like myself. Even though I knew that I had many blessings in my life, including a good marriage, I also knew that I was broken on the inside. Mike and I attended church regularly, and I listened intently hoping to find the freedom that I believed God offered through Jesus Christ. I tried to apply God's Word to my life and prayed for a healing of my self-esteem. Nothing seemed to make any real difference. Even if I felt hopeful for a time, my distorted truth would come crashing in on me. I don't think most people would have thought of me as unstable. To the contrary, I think most people thought well of me. It was only me that could not think well of myself. Oh sure, I was smart. I was a contributing professional teacher. But, I was ugly, in my point of view, and I could not get past that in my heart and emotions.

As I mentioned earlier, Mike was not big on giving compliments. His answer to my feelings of ugliness was that I should not care what other people think of me. What others thought should make no difference at all to me. That sounded so sweet in theory, but I couldn't change what I already believed to be true. Even if Mike had generously showered me with compliments about my great beauty in his eyes, I doubt if I could have believed him. I would not have trusted him to tell me the truth on this matter. Years later, as I think back, maybe he did try to give me compliments in the early years of our love and marriage. Maybe he gave up because I could not receive it even when he gave them sincerely. This is a possibility although it grieves me to consider it.

Love and marriage weren't the answer. Orthodontic braces weren't the answer. Lessons learned from church sermons and women's conferences didn't seem to hold the answer. Spousal pep rallies didn't seem to be the answer. I was desperate to find the answer. I hated my life because I hated my very self. I did not want to carry the ugliness and hurt from high school with me for the rest of my days on earth. I just could not do it, and I would not do it. I felt little hope, but I kept searching for the miracle that would change me on the inside. There had to be an answer for these feelings of ugliness and self-contempt. I just needed to find it.

Chapter 32

Before Mike and I married, we had talked about whether we wanted to have children as part of our lives. We both came from large families with seven children in each. He thought that he wanted to have children eventually but not right away. I told him that I had plenty of children at school in my role as a teacher. I also told him, honestly, that I did not think that I ever wanted to have children of my own. He wasn't worried about our differing views because he thought that I would come around to it eventually. It wasn't anything that we needed to decide on then. He just wanted to be newlyweds for a few years, and then we could make the kid decision later.

Besides the fact that children already filled my days at school, there were other legitimate and not so legitimate reasons that I was undecided about having our own babies. Some of these reasons I discussed honestly with Mike, but a few I held deep inside me. My honesty with Mike ended at the point where I could not fully reveal to him one of my biggest fears about having a baby.

As everyone knows when it comes to babies, there are no guarantees. There were no assurances that our children would look like him. I would even be happy if they had his mouth, and otherwise looked like me. One very real fear was that my children would look like me. What if they were born with fishy-looking lips and had to live their whole lives feeling ugly and bullied? I did not want to subject any child of mine to these same feelings that haunted me. Besides, would I even be able to love a child if he or she looked like me? I couldn't even like myself!

It didn't help that one of my friends at work had told me that babies always take on the strongest features of each parent. I wasn't sure if this was accurate information, but she already had one child, so she might know something that I did not know. It seemed to genetically make sense to me. I thought if this were true, any child of mine would have my mouth. I could not bear that thought!

As our married friends began to have babies we watched with mixed feelings. It seemed that, as in the jump-roping ditty, after love and marriage someone should come along with a baby carriage. Mike was comfortable waiting for me to come around on the topic, and I was comfortable avoiding my private trepidation about babies, especially a baby of mine.

We never argued or fought over the topic. It was not a tender topic between us. We just sort of drifted from one year to the next without making any decisions. My sister pointed out to me that not making a decision was actually making a decision. Many well-meaning people pointed out to us that we were exactly the kind of couple that should be having children to add quality to the gene pool. At least one friend of my parents said that we must be awfully selfish to be childless by choice. If only they could have known what was on my mind as they gave such kindly encouragement or tough judgment.

As I meandered through the best of my child-bearing years, Mike contentedly came along with me. Whenever I mentioned that maybe we should at least consider having a baby, he said that he was content with the way things were at the present. Although we were meticulous with our birth control measures, I knew that God was the ultimate Giver of Life and that He could certainly override any of our plans. That happened all the time! Right? Look around at all the unplanned pregnancies! I also knew that I didn't feel any strong mothering instincts beyond what I freely provided in my teaching job. Because Mike didn't bring any pressure to bear, I was content to leave well-enough alone. And, so the years ticked by....

Chapter 33

The passion of being newlyweds slowly faded into a warmer, deeper, more trusting love. Mike and I were happy as a couple working and saving towards our shared dream of building a home in the woods. Because we had no children, we were some of the lucky few who could take a tropical or sightseeing vacation at least once a year. Our friends with young children were occasionally envious of our lifestyle of freedom. They had their joys, too; they were just different from ours.

Although I tried to present a picture of contentment to those around me, I knew there was still a much damaged part of me on the inside. Mike tried to understand it, but he never fully could. Because he was able to lay aside the bullying that he endured during his early teens, he didn't understand why I could not do the same. He struggled to comprehend why others' opinions mattered so much to me. I seriously attempted to live my life with his viewpoint; that others' opinions about me didn't matter, but in the heart of me, I was still crying. I knew that I could never be complete, no matter how much he loved me, until I could accept myself. I decided that maybe I needed to get some professional counseling if I ever hoped to be made emotionally whole.

Although I don't remember how it transpired, I found the name of a small Christian counseling center in a city within an hour's drive of where we lived. I made the call to find out the cost and was told that they were not accredited by the state at that time, so my insurance would not cover any of the costs. This made for a sore spot between Mike and me. He thought if I needed to get counseling, at least I should find a counselor that would be partially covered by our insurance. I argued that I really wanted to see a counselor that held to my same Christian values and might help me find healing in God. Mike finally relented, just wanting me to be happy and to have my sad feelings behind us once and for all. With some of my own very ambiguous feelings, I called to make my appointment.

Because of my teaching schedule I made my appointment for an evening after a full day of teaching. I was extremely nervous on my long drive to the Center for Family Healing. I knew that I needed to take this step, but I dreaded having to lay my story on the line to a stranger. My only comfort was that the counselor represented herself as a Christian, and I believed that she should do me no harm.

After my arrival at the Center I had a short wait until my appointment. I so desperately wanted to be there, but I also desperately felt like bolting out the door. Sheer determination to find healing and wholeness kept me seated and waiting in the reception area. (In hindsight I know that the counselor was taking a few minutes to pray for me and our session.)

After just a few minutes, Lynda, the counselor invited me into her counseling room. She let me breathe (however shallowly!) for a few minutes as we introduced ourselves and made small talk. And then came the question that I hadn't exactly anticipated in these same words, "What are you here for?" I don't know what I was expecting she would say, but not that! Maybe I thought she would just beat around the bushes and eventually figure out my problem. I knew the whole reason I had come to see Lynda, and I had to find the courage to tell her aloud. Unless I was honest with the counselor, how could I hope to find hope? With sheer resolve I choked out the first words of my story. Lynda didn't seem to flinch or even bat an eye. She just listened and let me talk. Once the floodgate was opened the hurt and emotion poured forth, and she let me spew my painful story without much interruption. The hour went by too quickly and the main thing that I gleaned from our first session was that I should begin to "invite Jesus" into the hurt and sadness of all that I was feeling. I had never done that before. All my prayers relative to the topic had been more along the lines of "God, please, make it stop."

I also remember her commenting on the fact that I was telling her some horrible things that had happened to me, but I was trying to smile my way through it. She was curious about why I was trying to hide the pain behind a smiling façade. Even when I was tearful and obviously in deep pain, I was attempting to block my true emotions from my face. I couldn't tell her why that was, because I didn't know that I was even doing it. But I did know that I had spent years trying not to let others see the hurt inside of me, including my parents, siblings, and friends.

I made my next appointment and drove home with my mind in a total whirl of thoughts. There was so very much to think about. It felt like a good first step to healing, just having shared my story aloud to a caring and nonjudgmental professional. I tried to share with Mike about my session with Lynda, but I'm sure he felt overwhelmed. I know that I felt overwhelmed with trying to remember all that had been said. I don't believe that sleep came easily that night. I couldn't wait for my next appointment believing that the hardest part was behind me now.

During the week ahead while I anxiously waited for my next counseling session, I did start to "invite Jesus in" to my emotions and especially any feelings relative to my looks. I won't say that it changed the world for me, but I think it was a beginning step. At least my mind went somewhere else besides just feeling horrible about looking like a largemouth bass. It gave me another thought to think.

The week slowly passed, but finally came the evening of my second appointment with Lynda. I was nervous, but I also couldn't wait to get there and get started. Lynda wanted to spend much of the session talking about my family and the dynamics of my family tree. She wanted to talk about early memories and early disappointments. Frankly, I thought we were wasting our time and my money on this topic, but as a professional she knew that there were things to be discovered in the branches of my family tree.

Lynda believed that self-esteem is formed earlier in childhood and encouraged me to consider my relationship with my mother. She assigned me the task of interviewing my mother about our early years together. In doing so I found out some things that I hadn't known previously.

Counselor Lynda also wanted me to consider how things may have been different if I had included my parents, who more than likely loved me dearly, in the pain of my teen years and beyond. Lynda weekly modeled for me "inviting Jesus into" all of the aspects of my pain and loss.

While it took me some convincing to face my childhood reality, Lynda explained to me that it was quite likely in a family of seven children, with one child having special needs, that many of my emotional needs had not been met in early childhood. She felt that there were hurting parts of me that still needed comforting even as an adult. Although I didn't want to face this, it seemed to make reasonable sense to me. We had been well cared for physically, but with seven youngsters, how could parents possibly provide for each child's emotional needs? Lynda demonstrated to me how the adult Roseanne could emotionally hold and bring comfort to the little girl

Roseanne. It was something to consider and something that took practice, but I committed to do it to gain my healing.

At some point in the weekly counseling sessions, Lynda made me face my high school decision to lower my grades to avoid a valedictory speech or any recognition at my graduation. She also encouraged me to delve into my reasons for not wanting to have a baby. She felt that there were some HUGE losses in my life that I had never grieved appropriately for over the years. I had made decisions and ignored their impact on my life without allowing myself to grieve their loss. She found many issues that had been stuffed down deeply when they should have been honestly grieved in the light of day and truth.

On another occasion Lynda had me draw a picture of how I saw myself from a physical perspective. While I am a rather simplistic artist, I tried to comply. She then had me draw a picture of how I thought Jesus saw me in a physical sense. Again I tried, and managed slightly more than a stick-person perspective. She then had me hold the two pictures side-by-side. She asked me what I saw as the difference between the two pictures. I had trouble honestly answering, so Lynda pointed out the main difference that she saw between the two drawings. In the drawing of how I thought Jesus viewed me, I was smiling. In the view of how I saw myself, I was frowning. The shape and size of my lips and mouth were virtually the same in both drawings, but one had a smile and one had a frown. It gave me food for thought in the weeks ahead.

As she counseled, Lynda brought another aspect of the bullying and abuse into the light for me to consider. Although I did not understand what she was saying at the time and I found it hard to comprehend and believe, I have since begun to understand. She directed my attention to the huge and personal spiritual awakening that I had experienced in the years preceding our move to the new town and new high school. She pointed to the fact that spiritually I was alive and well and on fire for Jesus Christ. I was bold in the sharing of my faith and was willing to reach out to others with the love of Christ. I was not afraid to carry my Bible into the public school and take a stand for my Lord.

At the time of our counseling sessions, I did not know much about spiritual warfare or the constant battle between good and evil forces on planet Earth. If anything such talk made me afraid. I did not even like to think about demonic forces playing a role in the lives of everyday people, and especially in my life. Lynda believed and said in no uncertain terms, and from a Christian perspective, that what had happened to me had been spiritual. She discerned that what had happened in the physical had also happened in the spiritual; a battle had been waged against me. As I said, I did not really understand what she was saying because I was purposely blind to the spirit realm and warring spirits. At that time, I did not even want to acknowledge that possibility in my life.

In the years since those counseling sessions, I have learned a great deal about spiritual warfare and found that I have nothing to fear because I am in the care and keeping of Jesus Christ. I can talk about spiritual warfare and not feel afraid. I have also concluded that Lynda was right in believing that what had happened to me was a spiritual attack as well as an attack in the physical realm. The reason I know this is because my enemy and his demonic cohorts took me from a much on-fire and bold Christian teenager to a defeated, weak, wanting-to-blend-into-the-woodwork, hopeless teenager with nothing to offer to anyone. My enemy, satan, won the battle, and

I went into hiding for many years to come. He would NOT have wanted a strong, bold, fearless child of God to bring that living faith into a new high school environment. There were young lives to impact, and he did not want that to happen. Most people would acknowledge that high school is a critically important time for making life choices and decisions. I believe that satan did not want a positive, godly influence coming into my new high school. What I could not see or understand forty-some years ago is now clear and evident to me. I definitely lost the battle waged against me, but the war was not over yet.

After six counseling sessions, Lynda felt that we were ready to wrap things up and that I could begin to move on with my life. BEGIN was the operative word, from my point of view. I did not believe that I had arrived at healing as I had expected and hoped to do. I thought that I should have a weekly appointment for the next year or two. She felt that I was ready to move on with the help she had given me, with the understanding that I could come back in the future and continue the process with a professional as needed. Mike was just happy to stop the bleed in our checking account. At that point, I did not care about the cost of counseling but decided to go along with Lynda's recommendations and see where I ended up.

Seven years later I would return for six more sessions to deal with the baby decision and also with issues surrounding my relationship with my mom. Decidedly, that family tree did have its importance!

Chapter 34

After my counseling sessions ended, I was left on my own to begin to make application of what Lynda had shown me. It was enough to get me started and thinking in a new direction. Instead of just feeling ugly and unlovable, I could now invite Jesus into all of my sad, mad, or bad feelings. I had never really done this before. In the past it was more of a desperate plea for God to heal my emotions or help me not to think these ugly thoughts, or to stop the pain. It had always seemed that the ugly feelings of sadness and rejection were going to literally kill me, and in some ways they had killed me on the inside. How I felt about myself had robbed me of potential and self-confidence in my young adult life.

As I began to invite Jesus into my brokenness, I discovered that feelings of rejection would not kill me. I still didn't like them and wanted to avoid those hurtful emotions, but I realized I would not literally die from feeling them. The road ahead was long and winding, and I won't imply that it was easy. The wounds that I experienced, and the beliefs that I ascribed to because of the years of hurting words, were not something that I was going to get over quickly. In fact, just realizing that the healing would never be quick and miraculous was part of the healing process. I just wanted to be better and feel better about my looks. When I truly grasped the fact that this would not ever happen quickly and completely, I let go of that unrealistic wish and grabbed hold of a S-L-O-W and drawn out lifelong process. I had to let go of the hope of a miracle and face the fact that it was going to take a very long time to find my freedom.

On rare occasions I would return to that hope of a quick and miraculous healing. When our church had guest speakers or guest evangelists with healing ministries, I attended and went to the altar for special prayer when the opportunity was given. I would never say exactly what my prayer need was, but simply requested prayer for emotional healing or a special unspoken need. I figured that God knew what it was, and that was sufficient. The quick and supernatural fix that I was longing for never came. It became obvious that healing would not come to me this way. Because I had no apparent choice, I decided that I would accept that fact and take my healing day by day, one day at a time. What else could I do? It seemed the only thing I could do was to invite Jesus into my pain and into the healing of my broken heart. Even if it took forever....

Chapter 35

It still amazes me that I chose a profession that put me back into a school setting, my prior place of torment. Of course, I was not with the same grade or age level, not in the same school or even in the same town, but still I was back in school. I must have had enough positive school experiences prior to high school, and enough passion to work with special needs students, to keep me determined to become a teacher.

While teaching, both in special education and in regular education, I was able to observe bullying of all types—from subtle to blatant. Many times the child being bullied had something that made him stand out as different from his more typical peers. It may have been size, shape, hair color, a physical feature, inadequate cleanliness, attire, mental ability, or learning differences, to name just a few possibilities. At times it was none of those things but rather more of a personality difference such as shyness, a lack of confidence, or obvious self-esteem issues. Generally, the child being bullied was perceived to be different in some way or was made to believe that they were different from their peers. At times this was not true at all, as when a child was picked on because of their unique name. Who is to say what is typical anymore?

Bullying was one thing that I never tolerated in my classroom. In fact, when I saw it happening, I made it a point to come alongside the victim in no uncertain terms. I made it clear that I had been bullied in school and that it would not be tolerated on MY watch! Most young children looking at their teachers can barely imagine that they were once young children, let alone imagine that they had once been weak enough to be bullied. Whenever I spoke of this, I felt students studying me very carefully to see if I was telling them the actual truth. I know beyond all doubt that my students felt safe in my classroom and in my care.

One problem with bullying is that victims are not always in your classroom or in your personal care. It doesn't take long for most bullies to figure out that this is not something appropriate to do in front of grownups. The teachers and staff at school can try to prevent bullying, but bullies usually find ways to circumvent protective and compassionate adults. What happens on the school bus, or walking home, or on the far end of the playground, usually isn't found out by attentive and caring bus drivers, teachers, or parents. Bullies know this! I have overheard absolutely shocking words through my open classroom window when unaware students are on the playground. If there is no adult visually present or within likely earshot, students will say the cruelest and most vile things.

Unfortunately, not all school staff have the determined motivation to keep bullying from happening at school. While they may agree that it is wrong, it takes a lot of effort, time, and wisdom to follow through with a bully. Some professional and paraprofessional support staff just plain don't want to get involved with bullies. Besides the time and effort that it takes away from other things, they say that kids need to work it out between themselves or that victims need to learn to deal with it in one way or another. They may justify that there will always be bullies, so each person needs to learn how to deal with the bullies that they meet.

The vast majority of parents want the schools to deal with bullies. They are horrified to hear that their *sweet innocent* child might actually have a tendency toward being a bully. Most parents will work determinedly with the schools to avoid having their child labeled as such even in spoken words. Regrettably, there are some adult bullies who raise bullies of their own. When this happens, the children have a free-for-all with no parental intervention or discipline. This is a sad and inappropriate lack of parenting.

In recent years bullying has been a very hot topic in the national and world media. Cyberbullying has added new and ugly dimensions to an already serious life-impacting problem. I can't even imagine how much worse my life could have been had social media been a fact of my teenage life.

Much of the nation's media attention has focused on teens that have been bullied who have gender identity and sexual preference issues. Lives have been destroyed by cyberbullying on social media. Devastated teens have seen no possible end to their pain except suicide. I totally agree that these happenings are ugly and unacceptable in a supposedly civilized country, but I do not agree that bullying is a gay issue as some would like to claim. It happens every day to students all over the world who are perceived to be different in one way or another. Being gay or having gender identity issues is only one way to be perceived as different from one's peers.

Bullying is not a gay issue or a straight issue. It is a human issue. It impacts most of us in one way or another, and it will take all of us to make things better.

Part 2

The Rescue

Chapter 36

I will repay you for the years the locusts have
eaten...
Joel 2:25 [NIV]

During my third and fourth decades of life I
continued to find emotional healing by allowing Jesus
to help carry my pain. My marriage to Mike was
generally happy, and I was very much respected in
my profession as a teacher and in my community.
With the continuing emotional healing came a simple
confidence that had been lost for a very long time. My
self-confidence began to slowly return to me as Jesus
began to restore to me what the locusts had eaten, as
found in Joel 2:25. (Please put heavy emphasis on
slowly and began, because it was not something that
happened even as fast as at a snail's pace.)

I won't say that there weren't hurtful times when
I felt someone was making subtle fun of my looks or
the shape of my mouth. There still were hurtful
scenarios, both real and imagined, that weakened
me, but I was able to bounce back much more
quickly by using the skills that I had learned from
Lynda during her professional counseling. The main

and most useful skills were inviting Jesus into the pain and also allowing for the grief instead of fighting it. I now realized that the sadness would not kill me. No one likes to feel rejection, but in and of itself, it will not kill a person. That was a valuable discovery for me.

I was very pleased and hopeful for the growth I could see happening in me. I now believed that it was going to take a lifetime to heal, but I felt accepting of this just knowing that eventually I would no longer feel such deep pain over my looks and what had happened to me in high school.

Another huge factor in my gradual healing at this time was that I began to tell Mike current things that happened or words that had been spoken, and how I was feeling about them. In the past I hid all of my hurts from my parents, siblings, and friends so that I had to bear my grief totally alone. I would not speak of my pain even to people who obviously cared deeply about me. I could not put voice to the destruction. Once I got up the courage to tell Mike on a more regular basis, he could help me to see truth or error in my thinking and reactions. Just the act of telling him and allowing him into my feelings made a huge difference in my ability to get out of my broken pattern of thinking about myself. It made my incident-recovery-time much quicker. Instead of feeling broken for days, I may have felt sadness for only hours or minutes. The more I was able to voice my feelings to him the quicker I was able to emotionally recover. Insensitive words by others didn't bring me as low, and by sharing them with someone who I knew loved me, I didn't stay in the pit so long. I felt hopeful in my situation.

In a similar sense, when my parents (especially my mom) would bring up the topic, I was able to talk just a tiny bit about the hurt without running away from it at top speed. For her, it was a way to express her sadness for what had happened to me, as well as her guilty feelings that she hadn't known about it, or hadn't rescued me in some way. I saw her grief in it and felt obligated to reassure her that there had been nothing she could have done because she couldn't possibly have known. I hadn't allowed her to know. I felt badly that she felt badly, and so I was willing to talk to her in a very guarded way without revealing any specific details of how the bullying had played out. Even though I started to write this story while she was living, I knew that I would never allow her to read it or see it. And, so it was to be...

Sharing with my dad was even more complicated, in a sense. He usually referred to it as the "bad time" I had in high school or stated that I didn't really like high school after we moved. I have tried to explain to him that it was neither of those things. He had been picked on, in a small way, in grade school. But like Mike, he seemed able to move beyond it. His generally positive attitude no doubt helped him to not get stuck in the rejection. For him it was a temporary thing. Nonetheless, being able to speak to another caring human, on any level, helped me move closer to my goal of emotional wellness.

Chapter 37

During the years after high school, something had happened to me that I didn't see fully until thirty-some years later. I might have seen a change in me, and in fact, I might have even liked the change. But I didn't recognize or realize that it was a defense mechanism that I had taken on as part of my personality. I became a more hardened person. I was stronger in some ways, but this played out in terms that can have both positive and negative connotations. I lived with a strong personality that wasn't always perceived as a good thing. I developed a strong offense as my best defense. At times, I was referred to as feisty, ornery, hard, strong-willed, and I held tightly to a don't-mess-with-me attitude. I developed a keen and strong sense of justice and injustice.

My professional teaching friends knew that I would be the one who would speak up when necessary, and they often placed me in the lead and got behind me to follow (and push). I ended up on the teachers' union contract negotiations team for my colleagues for about twelve years. When there was a complaint or point of view that needed to be expressed, I was sought out to lead the charge. When people needed a letter of recommendation for anything, I was asked to contribute. When there was a disagreement with those in authority, I was asked to speak my piece. Because I was a professional in every sense, my opinion was generally valued by those in high places within our school district.

However, without intending to, I was headed in the exact opposite direction from the biblical advice in Chapter 1 of James (1:19–20), one of my favorite books of the Bible. I became quick to anger and quick to speak. I was almost always ticked off at somebody about something. There are likely situations of unfairness in any job or profession, but things seemed worse in our small rural community with its slim financial resources.

During this time of courageous front-lining, I also started giving school board presentations with my students on a regular basis. These were welcomed in a very positive way by the parents and school board members in the community. I was respected and had a name that was recognized by most people in my small town.

I became known as a teacher who would be strong in discipline and hold high expectations for my students. Parents either demanded me as their child's teacher or strongly opposed me. They knew that I would ask much of myself and much of their child. They knew that I was not a person to mess with, and not all parents wanted that for their child or for themselves.

This very strong-willed part of me had likely been in my DNA from conception, but it certainly went into hiding during high school and the years beyond. It came flaring back as a strong mechanism of defense! It was as if I determined that it would be better if I hurt you before you had the chance to hurt me. I never actually said or even thought that, but I suspect that was my emotional motivation. I was strong and nobody was going to hurt me again, not if I could help it.

This strength and determination had benefits and drawbacks. It just depended on what the circumstance was and who was judging the situation. In and through these situations I became a strong leader in my school!

Fortunately, I didn't necessarily need this defense with Mike at home. Truthfully, he rarely gave me reason to use it with him. He knew that I was a strong woman with a good vocabulary. While we had the normal highs and lows of a longstanding married life, I did not often perceive injustice coming from Mike. I didn't feel any need to hurt him before he had the chance to hurt me.

Sad to say, but in my family of origin and with my siblings, I was thought of as the sibling with the hard edge who would say what I thought, very directly, with little regard for anyone's feelings. I am not proud to say that now. At some points in time I was proud to think that I was the "feisty" one, to put it nicely. Another way to describe me would be to say that I had become mean and inconsiderate. I did not want to be hurt so I would hurt others first.

I never set out to become this way, and when I discovered what I had really become, I was rather appalled. Hurting others would be the exact opposite of my heart's wish. Hard-heartedness was not what I wanted to have as my defense. It crept up on me over time, and I did not for many years fully comprehend it. Thirty-some years after high school I began to see this ugly, hurtful side of my personality. With the slow, drawn-out process of emotional healing came a clarity of who I had become and how I needed to change.

At that time we were involved in a small, nondenominational church in our community. Authenticity was stressed, with the idea that we all had flaws, sins, and secret pasts before God intervened in our lives. We were encouraged to take our masks off and be real with our brothers and sisters in Christ. Being part of this church allowed me, for the very first time, to begin to hint aloud, outside of my immediate family, about the hurtful times in my past. I was never specific about what had happened, but talked in generalized terms about the bullying and pain in my past. Of course, many other people could relate and had aspects of the same story in their lives.

As I began to slowly reveal some small bits of the truth about who I really was, I also became willing to acknowledge that I had become a hardened, don't-mess-with-me type of person. I began to concede and confess that some of those toughened, cynical parts of my heart needed to be changed. In fact, I began to see that what I thought was a strong, butt-kicking woman was really a still-hurting defensive little girl on the inside. The strength I thought I saw was in fact real, but also distorted into a self-protective measure to cover up the enduring pain. It seemed the pendulum had swung too far in the other direction.

I knew that I needed God to soften the hardened parts of me and to continue to heal the little girl inside the grown woman...me.

Chapter 38

Thinking back to my much-earlier counseling at the Center for Family Healing, I remembered that Lynda had told me that God would continuously bring me back to deal with my pain in an ever-deepening, ever more healing way. In public education we call that the *spiral curriculum*.

In school, teachers don't just teach their students about verbs once. Rarely is there ever a once-and-done lesson in school or in life. As an example, teachers continue to teach students about verbs but each time in a deeper way. Something is always added to intensify the learning. First, students learn about *action* verbs, then *being* verbs, then the various tenses of verbs, then about *helping* and *linking* verbs, and then *phrasal* verbs, etc. The curriculum spirals back to verbs in an ever more complex way over the course of a school year, and also over all the years of a child's education. One is never really done with verbs until maybe high school graduation, unless one takes college English. Then the spiral continues to be reviewed.

In the ensuing years after my counseling with Lynda, I found that what she predicted was going to be all too true. I did not like it that God brought me back to the pain over and over and over and over again. Each time He did there were new things to consider, more to understand, and more healing to be done. My emotions were being healed in what seemed to me like the tiniest little fragments imaginable. I believed it was going to be a 'til-death process, and there was no way to speed things up, much as I wanted and would have preferred. But, God knew what He was doing in me!

At one time earlier on in my healing process, in my attempt to find quicker relief from my pain, I attended a special service where the visiting evangelist was supposedly able, by the power of the Holy Spirit, to speak prophetically over a person's life. Of course I wanted him to pray for me. What he said over me was that he saw my life as a jigsaw puzzle that had been smashed on the floor, with the pieces flying in all directions. But, God was going to bring the pieces all back together again to make me whole.

I wasn't sure what to make of the whole experience, but it certainly seemed like these words were true. (Maybe those same words would be true for every life.) It seemed that God was in the process of putting the pieces of my life back together—in a long, slow process. Bit by bit, piece by piece, He was bringing me back to the pain so that I could deal with it in an ever deeper, more complex, and intensified way. I guess God believes in the *spiral curriculum*, too, at least in the processing of injury in my life! Maybe for each of us there is no once-and-done in the healing, sanctifying process of our lives.

Chapter 39

The healing within me was almost always driven by the Holy Spirit and my desire to get well emotionally. Something, large or small, would trigger the pain of the past in me. As I felt the sting and began to turn to God to help me deal with it, He always provided some morsel of hope to keep me moving forward. Maybe it would be a song on the Christian radio station, a paragraph in a book, a sermon in church, a life group discussion, a word of encouragement from a stranger, or a scripture from the Bible. Some seemingly insignificant tidbit would move me ahead in the smallest of ways toward wholeness.

Sometimes those tidbits came quietly and privately in my spirit. Other times they came like a hurricane to interrupt me unexpectedly. Sometimes the hurricane was precipitated by a perceived enemy, and other times it was brought on by close and intimate friends.

Within our small community church we became extremely close friends with a handful of people. They became for us our spiritual inner circle. Both Mike and I shared in these deep relationships. As we grew in our friendships I begin to reveal more and more truth about my life and my past pain. No one seemed to like me less when I was honest even in small ways.

On one occasion, at a spa party in our home with three of my best and closest church girlfriends, the question was asked, "What is your one physical feature that you absolutely hate?" I had an "OH, NO!" moment when I realized I was expected to answer that question, too, between intimates. I listened to what the other three had to say and realized that the body-feature that they most hated about themselves was actually not even true about them. The friend with the L-O-N-G, skinny legs hated her "short, stubby legs." Another dear friend hated her hair, which was a beautiful silver with a flattering cut that both men and woman found very attractive on her. The third friend hated her chin line. What chin line? Not one of the other three of us had even noticed it!

The whole time I was listening to my dear friends talk so casually about their self-perceived worst feature, I was wondering how I could BOLT from my own home to avoid answering the question! Emotionally, I felt like a trapped animal. I wanted to escape, but there seemed to be no way out! I couldn't run from my own house when I was the hostess, could I? Finally after several uncomfortable minutes of a delaying, "I—can't—do—this," I was able to spit it out that it was my lips and the shape of my mouth. The three of them just stared at me with the look of, "WHAT are you talking about?" They professed that the only thing they had ever noticed about my mouth was my large and beautiful smile! I didn't know what to make of their comments other than to assume they were not really being honest with me. In my heart, though, I knew that we each had been honest with the other three, so why would they lie to me? Were they speaking truth to me?

Again, God had spiraled me back to the pain. To face it, to feel it, to grieve it, to accept it, to voice it, and to trust that I would not die from sharing it aloud with my closest friends. Overcoming the fear of saying it aloud that evening brought me another small piece of healing in my soul and spirit. Over the years, God continuously brought me back to my pain to deal with it in an ever-deepening, ever more healing way.

Chapter 40

Friends are some of the very best parts of my life. Over the years, I made the discovery that it's not the number of friends that a person has but the level of intimacy that a person shares with those friends. Even one close intimate friend is truly enough. More than one is a bonus! (I have voiced that dozens of times, to all of my students, in my years as their teacher.)

Back at the high school where my bullying began, I was not without friends. As I have previously mentioned, I did have a few close friends that no doubt helped me to literally survive the ordeal. Although we enjoyed each other's company, we have not maintained those friendships in the years since high school. We occasionally caught up with each other in the first years after graduation, but our ties certainly did not become lifelong. I cared very much for those friends at the time, but we weren't able to talk about the obvious "elephant in the living room" of my life. It's likely that none of us had the maturity to move the conversation into those scary, dark, and way-too-personal places. Ignoring the elephant was so much easier!

The situations and settings of life naturally bring people together for potential friendships. Roommates in college, friends of roommates living down the hall, other students in a grad class, tenants in an apartment building, colleagues at work, co-parishioners in a church, and neighbors on a block all provide us opportunities to befriend another person.

In the years after high school I became very guarded in making new friendships. I took my time deciding whether any potential friends could be trusted not to hurt me. I have found over the years that most of my closest friends are "flawed" in some way. I have no friends that are raving beauties, and if I did, I likely wouldn't totally trust them. Even those who are very attractive in physical appearance have some issue that makes them seem flawed, even if it's just an ongoing struggle with their weight.

I'm not saying that I purposely sought out other "underdogs", but that is what I have ended up with as my very best and lifelong friends. Even more important than having friends with flaws has been the importance of having friends with faith. While all of my dearest friends are in various and sundry places in their spiritual walks, all of them are walking in faith and looking toward a heavenly future. God is pursuing them and winning their hearts, just as He is mine! Our shared faith allows us to walk our pasts out into the light of day and get healed by the One who can bring genuine healing.

Having flawed friends makes me feel safer. What sticks and stones can they throw at me? They likely have felt the sting of hurtful words, which may not have broken their bones, but have broken or damaged their hearts. Over the years of shared pillow talk in the dorm, days at the beach, or hours over steamy cups of coffee, I have found that most of my friends have an injured place in their heart caused by the careless words of a bully, or at best, an inconsiderate peer or spouse. I'm not saying their pain makes me feel better about myself, so that I can be their friend, but it does help me to know that I am not the only one who has felt rejection and hurt. We have a shared pain that we can understand because we have all felt it.

In long conversations with these friends, I find that I still struggle to be direct with my insecurities and hurts. I am afraid to make myself vulnerable even with my very best friends. This is also true with family members, who obviously love me, too. I hint and hem and haw around the topic, but I just have trouble saying the words that caused me such pain. Even in talking about this book I remained vague about the specifics of the bullying. It's only the most courageous friends that have backed me into a corner and waited expectantly and patiently to hear what has caused me so much pain over the years. I appreciate those who've forced my issue, not to hurt me, but because they loved me. Every time I have been able to voice the specific details of my painful past, I have found another measure of true healing.

Chapter 41

In the forty-some years since high school, emotional healing has come tip-toeing into my life when and where I never thought possible. The answer that I was crying out for desperately, was slowly but surely coming my way. I had wanted instantaneous healing of all of the hurt, grief, and brokenness. It wasn't to be, no matter how much I wept and begged for God to do something to fix me.

All manner of His tiny touches to my life were, and still are, working together for my wholeness and good. Time may heal all wounds, but time alone did not bring me healing. It took an uncountable number of tiny steps and millimeters of progress in the direction of healing to bring me to where I am today. Little pieces of the puzzle were being glued into place, making the picture of my life easier to see. In earlier pages of this book I have hinted at some things that brought me small measures of healing, little by little, and step by step.

Nobody was coaching me on how to bring about my healing any faster. But, I discovered quite unexpectedly and accidentally a powerful catalyst that moved me forward in significantly larger strides.

Attention, Reader! This discovery was HUGE! The fortuitous discovery? God's word about me and to me!

I remember an evening in late winter when I was driving home alone on a dark and gloomy road. I had been wounded by the words of a supposed friend and colleague. At this time in my healing process, a situation like this would normally have taken me days to shake off, get over, and to move beyond.

Mike and I were going to be leaving on vacation, and all I could think of was this extra suitcase of garbage that I was going to be dragging along with me. I did not want to ruin our vacation with my sadness and introspection. I knew I would have trouble explaining it to Mike, and I didn't even want to try. I did not want to ruin our vacation trip with my ongoing emotional issues, but I felt helpless against my feelings.

As I was driving I started praying aloud in the car. It was dark, remember? And I was on a lonely road. As I prayed, I started praying scripture. I was saying things like, "God, You made me, and You go before me. You are for me. You are my Refuge and my Strong Tower. You are a Shelter and a Shield. In my pain, I run to You. You have made me the head and

218

not the tail. I am victorious in You. You go before me, and You hem me in. You are my rear guard. You are my rescue and the One who lifts my head."

As I continued on the road toward home I realized that I was feeling an unexpected peace in my spirit. I was no longer feeling the sickening agitation that always went along with these feelings of rejection and emotional injury. Something BIG had happened!

I do believe that the something BIG was in the spiritual realm, beyond human vision and perception. I believe my words, or should I say God's word spoken by me, let good defeat evil. Angels were battling and winning a victory against demons. I was amazed and excited and HOPEFUL about this discovery! By the time I arrived home, I had moved beyond my broken self and knew that I could take one less piece of baggage with me on our vacation.

This was a BREAK-THROUGH of major proportion! For me, it was just the beginning of many more opportunities to speak the word of God into my life. The speed of my healing accelerated greatly once I made this discovery! It was time to move beyond the pain and let God be the lifter of my head. He had made me to be a victor and not a victim. I was onto something big and I knew it!! God had shown me a new weapon to use in my fight. It was free and available, and He gave me full access to it!

From that point on, when the largemouth bass would make its presence known in my mind and heart, I had a strategy to deal with it. Because it was a new discovery for me, I didn't usually think of it first or immediately. My old ways of handling the pain were my default setting. But, with practice and the resulting quicker relief from emotional injury, I began to run to God's word faster and faster. It truly brought me comfort every single time. It no longer took days, but sometimes only minutes, to feel relief and peace. I began to understand the power of the word of God. Not just because someone told me it was powerful, but because I had experienced it for myself! I felt the change in my spirit!

I was not one who could memorize scripture very easily or for long term remembering. As a child, I could memorize my Sunday school Bible verse and hold it in my memory just long enough to get a sticker or a small prize. After proving my success in memorizing it, I would let it slip away just as quickly. Likewise, I was never one who could retain the location of the verse in the Bible either. But, in the grand scheme of things, I had been reading and hearing the Bible being read for decades. If I didn't know the exact location of the verse, or didn't have the words exactly correct, for the most part I understood the idea of the verse and could give a rough approximation of many verses.

Psalm 139 [NIV] was a chapter that was very familiar to me. In the past, whenever I read it, I would feel hopeful but also be somewhat unbelieving of all that it said to me and about me. As I began to use this new strategy of speaking scripture to myself, many familiar verses would come to mind. Maybe I didn't have the exact wording, but I knew what God had said to me in various parts of this scripture passage. In a way I was confirming His words to me, but I also thought that I was reminding Him of what He had said to me. I often said, "God, You said this about me." I accepted that He already knew what He had said, but I wanted to let Him know that I knew and wanted Him to remember, too.

Once I made this discovery about using God's word to bring me peace, relief, and emotional healing, I was well on my way to becoming a whole person again. I knew that I no longer had to be burdened under the ugliness and brokenness of my earlier experiences. It wasn't that I no longer could have my feelings hurt; I was hurt many times. But I had found a way to slough off the pain without letting it seep deeply into my heart. I would no longer be forever broken!

Chapter 42

With my "discovery" and more consistent practice of using God's word to bring me comfort, I gained a bold confidence that had been missing for a very long time. I was much less fearful of what people could do to me with their words or implications. I didn't live with the suspicion that others were always talking about me or my looks. And, if they were, so be it. It no longer seemed to matter as much to me. If they had an opinion of me that was negative or hurtful, I wouldn't likely be able to change it anyway. I no longer felt the need to try to figure out what others were saying about me or if it could somehow be relative to my fishy looks. I began to lose my obsession about my mouth and my lips. If it seemed that someone was purposely being mean, with the intent to harm, I more often was able to brush it off with reasonable speed without letting it become a part of who I was as a person.

With my new confidence came opportunities that I would have never considered in the past. I became the Missions Director at my church, which meant that I had to stand in front of the entire congregation once a month to do a missions presentation. I was also a key player in organizing an annual Missions Convention at the church. God helped me greatly in these situations every time, but the emotional healing that He was granting was the biggest part of my ability to even take on these tasks.

This led to many other bold steps because I could always look back and say, "Well, if I could do that, then—" Although I would always feel the ahead-of-time jitters, I grew to enjoy public speaking and presentations. Once I actually began talking, the jitters mostly left, and I was free to go on with determined resolve. My first thoughts were no longer about if someone might think I was ugly or looked like a fish, duck, or lizard. I was no longer bound by those cords of emotional death. At times, while speaking, a destructive thought would come to mind and tempt me to lose my train of thinking. When this happened I had to mentally toss it off to God to handle it, and He always did.

Through all of those years of pain since high school, I felt I had a story to share that might help others in my same or a similar situation. I knew a book would be part of that, even if written for my eyes only. But, I also believed there would be opportunities to actually verbalize my story. I had held my secret inside for so long, not even sharing with my dearest friends or loving family members. I believed that someday it would need to be spoken aloud and in a variety of situations.

At this same time in my life, a dear and persuasive friend was teaching me that bringing even horrifying things into the light of day made them seem less scary and traumatic. When I was deeply troubled by something (anything!), she would press me hard to voice it. She assured me that our enemy satan (lower-case intended, once again) loved to have us keep secrets in the darkest parts of our hearts and minds. Once spoken, these horrifying thoughts held less power over us. She had me test that on a regular basis, and I found it to be true. Once voiced, even scary, ugly, or humiliating things have less power in the mind and emotions. For a person who has held a lot of secrets close to the heart, voicing them can really be a tough thing to do.

In one very confident moment I called the leader of a local faith-based girls club. I told her that I had a story to share with her middle school girls that I thought would be helpful and encouraging to them. I expected a rousing "YES!" Her response was that they would consider it and maybe place me on their calendar sometime down the road. I felt disappointed and also was afraid I would lose my motivation when the time came. I was ready NOW, but it was not to be in my time frame. Once I released it to God I knew that if it was meant to be, I would get a callback when the time was right.

I had to wait awhile, but lo and behold, the call came! I was nervous, but also ready to put voice to my story in front of a group of curious middle school girls. I discerned that I needed to take a close friend along who would pray for me as I spoke. I invited a friend that I knew loved me dearly but had never heard my story with all of its ugly, painful details. Besides the group of girls there would also be two or three adult leaders who I knew in varying degrees, although not necessarily as close friends.

On the evening of my big reveal I was nervous, but I was also ready to say what I had come to say. Opening my mouth so the first words could be spoken was one of the hardest parts. Once opened, I was at a point of no return! Still, the most challenging part was when I actually had to say "largemouth bass" aloud in referencing myself in front of this group of people. And, not just once, but I had to say it repeatedly throughout the presentation.

When I was finished, the group was quiet but appreciative. There were girls and leaders present who could totally relate to what I had experienced. I knew that would be the case. Our culture is saturated with bullying and sarcasm, and these were middle-schoolers after all! I did not stick out like a sore thumb. There were other hurting people in the room, and I was blessed to be able to share some of the secrets that were leading to my recovery and healing. **The most important one was using God's own words to tell me who I am to Him and who He is to me**.

As tough as this was, my presentation that night was one of the top-ten-most-healing things that I have ever done. I realized once again that unspoken painful secrets are strong captors. I wanted to be fully released from the hurt that had held me prisoner for so very long.

Chapter 43

I knew many more opportunities would come along to share my story aloud. I believed that with each time I did, it would become easier for me. Truthfully, it became very easy to share a *generalized* story of bullying and not fitting in, because that is true for so many young people. Even many adults remember similar pain from their pasts when they felt rejected, alone, or ostracized from the larger group. But, to this day, it remains at least somewhat difficult for me to get into the specifics and say aloud to myself and to others the words "largemouth bass." That continually surprises me because I know how very far I have come in the healing process.

When speaking those words "largemouth bass" no longer causes me even a hint of discomfort or dread, I will know that I have found total and complete healing. There will be no more scab to break open. I will be scarred, yes, but faded scars generally are not painful. They are just a remaining mark to show that something harmful has happened in the past. I believe I will carry my scars forever, part of who I am and always will be, but no longer painful.

Every five or ten years, when I realize that my graduating class is holding a reunion, I consider whether that would be something I would want to attend. At one point I expressed that I would certainly know, beyond any shadow of doubt, that I was truly whole if I could attend a reunion of my graduating class and survive without being emotionally injured. On more confident days I firmly believed that I could come away unscathed. (It should be noted that I have attended the class reunions of my former high school, my "old" school from which I had moved away. My classmates there have graciously invited and welcomed me with open arms!)

At a reunion, would I expect people to apologize or be sorry for what they had done to me? Would they even know or feel culpable for what they had done? Would I see what a mess their lives had turned out to be and celebrate that I had a better life overall? I don't have the answers to these questions, and I don't even want to waste time or energy considering them. They don't really matter in my life anymore. (Ironically, while writing this portion of the book, I received the invitation to my 40th Class Reunion in the mail!) To this point I have had no desire to return to the high school of my graduation. Someday I may;

but for now, it seems unimportant. I have nothing that I need to prove to my peers from high school or to myself. What's done is done, and under the amazing grace of Jesus Christ.

Chapter 44

My husband Mike has pointed out to me that when there is a vehicular accident that involves one or more vehicles, each party is considered by the courts to be some degree responsible. He says the minimum responsibility for involvement is 15% even if you are sitting in a parked car. My heart doesn't necessarily agree with the fairness of that, but Mike says it's the way the judge and jury will rule in any accident investigation for liability.

In my story, I had not considered that I was in any way responsible for what had happened to me in high school and in the years that followed. With encouragement from friends in my faith-based life group, I decided to consider my part in the events that played out. Surprisingly, I was able to see that although **I was a victim**, my reactions to the events likely gave me a role. That is NOT to say that I was guilty, accountable, or to blame for what happened. But, had I reacted differently, the outcome may have been very different.

As I started to brainstorm what my role may have been in what happened to me, I made a realistic list. Most of my responsibility centered on keeping the secret and carrying the shame alone. At the time, and for decades to follow, I did not voice my hurt to teachers, family, or friends. I lived in denial of my obvious pain. I kept quiet and hid within myself, locking others out of the hurting places.

Although I don't know if I could have at the time, I did not stand up to the bullies in any way. I did not speak up for myself or confront them. People who know me now find that extremely hard to believe, but at the time I did the only thing I knew to do. Fight or flight? I only knew how to flee! In so doing, I did not willingly participate in the normal activities of high school. I allowed myself to be cheated out of what might be considered some of the more enjoyable experiences of youth.

And sabotaging my success and grade point average? I was definitely responsible for making that choice. I had my reasons for why I did it, and they seemed perfectly sensible to me at the time. Good choice? Probably not, but I was the one who made that decision. Thankfully, my college and professional careers have not been seriously hampered by my "permanent record" from high school.

From a spiritual perspective, I don't believe that I ever truly asked God about what I should do at the time the bullying was happening. I only asked Him to make the bullying and the pain stop. It's possible that I did ask Him, but I don't remember ever doing so.

Some might argue that by living and walking in fear and seriously contemplating suicide, I was sinning. Yes, in truth, those are biblical sins, but I certainly did not understand satan's desire for my mind at that time in my young life. I was responsible for my thoughts and mindset, but I did not understand how to take my thoughts captive from a spiritual perspective. (2 Corinthians 10:5/Romans 12:2/1 Peter 5:8)

After some serious contemplation about owning my share of the situation, I had to admit that I did play a role. Although I was a victim in every sense of the word, my reactions likely impacted the outcome at some point, whether in the situation or in the years that followed.

A friend who loves me dearly asked me if I would handle things differently now, knowing what I know. I can't say, because I don't know. Rightly or wrongly, I believe I did the best that I could at the time. I was too weak to fight alone, and I didn't engage anyone to help. In a similar situation, next time, would I do better? I certainly hope so. Holding secrets and not asking for help are two sure ways to be defeated in every potential way—physically, mentally, emotionally, spiritually, and relationally. Victims need to somehow find a voice and find an advocate! Trying to go it alone is a surefire way to lose any battle!

Chapter 45

Anyone who has walked a Bible-based path of faith knows that forgiveness is a key theme found throughout both the Old and New Testaments. In the Old Testament forgiveness was achieved through the blood of animals sacrificed according to the requirements of the Law. In the New Testament forgiveness is found with repentance through the sacrificial blood of Jesus Christ. The Bible holds dozens of references to forgiveness. It is God's nature to forgive, and He expects it of His children. The Bible even says that we will be forgiven as we forgive others (Matthew 6:14–15). As we recite the Lord's Prayer, we ask God to forgive us our debts, or trespasses, as we forgive others' theirs (Matthew 6:12). The apostles Mark (11:25) and Luke (6:37) concur that this is what Jesus had indeed said to them when He was on the earth.

Even though I knew what the Bible had to say, it was a slow process to even reach the point of willingness to forgive those who had purposefully harmed me by their words. God brought me around to actual forgiveness just a little bit at a time. He wanted my obedience, but He also knew my wounded spirit would need some time. He gave me much grace as I struggled to reach the point where I was ready to even consider forgiveness.

Forgiveness isn't the same as forgetting what has happened. It is not excusing others for what they have done. It is making a conscious decision to do what God asks us to do. With my mind, I knew that God expected obedience from me in the area of forgiveness, but in my heart, I wasn't ready when it came to granting it to the perpetrators. My answer on that for many years was, "NO, I can't," or "NO, I won't."

In the early years after high school I had absolutely no desire to forgive. I was hurting and believed that those who had hurt me had no right to be forgiven. They hadn't asked me to forgive them, and I didn't expect that they would ask, even if I ever did see them again. I wasn't ready to let them off for what they had done to me. In fact, if anything, I wanted them to pay for it in some way. Obviously there was no way for that to happen, so instead I held my anger and unforgiving ways inside, along with the emotional pain that was already there.

The reader may recall that my brother-in-law did attempt to apologize years after he married my sister.

It was awkward for both of us, and my lame response was a hasty OK because I really didn't want to talk about it. Whether I forgave him or not, I can't say. I just decided to move on with it because he was now in the family, he wasn't going anywhere soon, and I loved my sister. I accepted his apology on some level, but I can't say whether it was true forgiveness on my part.

One of my dearest friends has frequently said that being unforgiving is like drinking poison and hoping someone else will die. (Likely not originally her thought, but a truism, nonetheless.) Being unforgiving eats you up on the inside, while the other person, or people, have no idea that you are even hurt or mad or sad. And literally, they often don't care or wouldn't care if they did know! I became an expert at drinking poison and hoping someone else would die!

Over the course of many years, and finally only through a sheer desire and determination to obey God on this, I moved toward making the decision to forgive. I think I slowly came to the realization that, ultimately, not forgiving was hurting me. I began to acknowledge that for my own health and wholeness, it was time. I needed to obey God and forgive. In order to do this, it was essential for me to name names and state their perceived "crimes" against me. I never did this publicly, of course, but in my quiet times with God. I sometimes did it in my head, or with my spoken voice, and sometimes as a list on paper. For those whose names I didn't know or remember, I still had the images of their jeering faces in my mind.

Forgiveness, for me, was not a once and done prospect. I committed to forgiving those who had harmed me, but I had to continue to commit to it. I had to keep bringing it back to God. I would give it to Him but then pick it up again to hold on to myself. I needed to let go and forgive over and over again. Each time the letting go became easier to do. I had to acknowledge that God was big enough to carry all of it, and that I did not need to keep picking it up. He wasn't setting it down for me to pick up, so why was I reaching to take it back out of His hands? Even now, at rare times, I need to remind myself that I have fully forgiven those who bullied me, and it is complete, by God's grace.

On some level, I suppose that I also had to forgive myself for my role in the situation or my reaction to it over the course of time. Although I was alone in my pain and did the best that I could at the time, I had some level of responsibility for how I reacted to the pain. A victim? YES! Without a doubt! But, if I had taken a stand against the bullies, told someone, or sought help, things might have played out differently. The good news is that it was generally much easier to forgive myself than those who had intentionally caused me pain.

The big exception to that generalization was that it was not easy to forgive myself in the area of sexual impurity. In my attempt to feel OK about myself and my perception of how I looked, I, like many people, had "looked for love in all the wrong places." As I stated earlier, purity isn't just what you do with your body, it is a heart attitude and state of mind. Purity isn't about how far you can go but how innocent you can stay.

In our modern age most people wouldn't think twice about my choices. While my parents didn't really say much on the topic of purity, it was assumed, and I did know what God and the Bible had to say about it. In Ephesians 5:3, it says our lives should not even have a hint of sexual immorality. In 1 Corinthians 6:18, we are told to "flee from sexual immorality. All other sins that a person commits are outside of the body, but whoever sins sexually, sins against their own body." In our sex-crazed modern world, the masses try to deny that truth, but God's laws are undeniable and unchanging. My body, mind, and spirit all knew the truth.

It took me many years to finally forgive myself, even long after I was a married woman. At one time I tried to make a confession to a minister that hardly knew me. He didn't seem even remotely shocked by what I told him, and it did nothing in helping me to forgive myself. I think I was expecting (or hoping for) him to assign me some tough acts of penance, but he did not.

Like much of my healing, self-forgiveness came slowly over time. It came as I talked things honestly through with my closest friends. I found that most people have regrets of some sort for things they have done, or not done, and that we all need grace, from each other and from God. God's grace is free to us because of the high price paid by His Son, Jesus. I am so thankful for that, and for authentic loving friends who weren't (and aren't) afraid to enter into the darkest corners of my secret "rooms." These friends helped me with the self-forgiveness that needed to happen along my path to full healing.

Reading the Bible on my own, hearing sermons at church, and listening to Christian radio songs about forgiveness, helped me to understand the magnitude of what I was doing by forgiving others and myself. I was coming back into a right standing with God. Not that forgiveness saved me, but it was pleasing to God, and it was His will for my life.

Had I died without forgiving the bullies, would I have missed out on heaven for my unwillingness to forgive? I don't believe so. My trust was in the saving grace and blood of Jesus Christ, not in my ability or readiness to forgive others. But, I know that I am mentally and emotionally more healthy because of my obedience to Jesus. He wants only good for His children, and forgiveness is a part of His provision of good things for each of us.

Chapter 46

On the way to emotional wholeness I discovered a book in our church's library that shouted for my attention. As a volunteer helping with the weekly cleaning, I ran headlong into a devotional called *Battlefield of the Mind: 100 Insights That Will Change the Way You Think* (Meyer, 2005). While cleaning that day I signed out the book. From my perspective, this could not wait until Sunday morning.

I already knew from reading the Bible that "as a (wo)man thinks, so (s)he is" (Proverbs 23:7) and that we are admonished to think about noble, lovely, right, admirable, pure, excellent, and praiseworthy things (Philippians 4:8). I also knew that in the Bible, satan is compared to a roaring lion, looking for someone to devour (1 Peter 5:8), and that we are reminded to stay alert to that fact. Our enemy often triumphs as we wrestle with our thoughts (Psalm 13:2). As he tries to defeat us in our thinking, we are told to be transformed by the renewing of our minds (Romans 12:2).

This amazing devotional, authored by Joyce Meyer, was a life-changer for me, and I have since purchased it to share with others. As a reader works through one hundred days of the devotional, he or she slowly comes to grasp the power of satan's lies and the strongholds in his or her own life. But, the reader is not left hopeless and defeated because Joyce also makes the truth of God's power and the ability to choose one's own thoughts abundantly clear. As I read and journaled through the daily devotionals, I realized that what I chose to think about and dwell on was within my power to control. When a negative, destructive, or unsettling thought came to mind, I had a choice in how I dealt with it. I could hang on to it and chew on it mentally. Or I could take the thought "captive" (2 Corinthians 10:5) and give it to God. When I "ran to Jesus" or called on God, He was there, ready and willing to help me change my thought patterns. I found it shocking at how quickly a disturbing thought could be replaced by a sense of peace when given directly over to God.

Breaking old habits takes time and effort. I have heard that it takes twenty-one days to break old habits and establish new ones. Considering my years of destructive thinking and self-loathing, I'm grateful that the book had 100 daily devotions on the topic. Twenty-one days would have been sorely insufficient. One hundred days helped me begin to establish new patterns. Joyce Meyer also has a full length book called *Battlefield of the Mind: Winning the Battle in Your Mind* (1995). But for me, the day-to-day devotional was perfect with its quick-read format. I often stayed on a specific devotional for several days as I worked to mentally and emotionally process the ideas. I then began to apply them practically in my life. The more I practiced taking negative thoughts captive, the better I began to feel about myself and my looks.

Along the same lines of taking my damaging thoughts captive, I learned that praise and worship went a long way in getting my eyes off of me and onto the One True God that was far more worthy of my attention. The Bible tells us to put on the garment of praise for the spirit of heaviness (Isaiah 61:3). I found that obedience to this worked amazingly well. Listening to recorded Christian music helped, from the radio or another format, but I found it much more effective to actually use my own mind, heart, and voice to speak or sing praises to God, in all three forms of His Trinity. While singing songs of praise and worship, my brain and emotions couldn't help but go to the noble, lovely, right, admirable, pure, excellent, and praiseworthy things (Philippians 4:8).

Do I always do that automatically? No! Sometimes it takes me awhile to even realize that my mind is headed down a negative path. And sometimes, I am lazy about doing what's best for me, and I let myself sit on the pity-pot for a while. But, once I realize it and get tired of sitting there in self-pity, I know what to do to change the course. Practice makes perfect? I'm not there yet, but I am well on my way! Praise the Lord for that! And for His help in finding the right resources on my journey to emotional wellness!

Chapter 47

Some readers might draw the mistaken conclusion that my healing came through the power of a positive attitude or positive thinking. Ultimately, I did learn the value of a positive attitude because my dad was a consistent teacher who modeled optimistic living his whole life. When I was younger my dad occasionally said that I lived my life by Murphy's Law. I don't know who poor Murphy was, but his name is miserably attached to the old adage that "anything that can go wrong, will go wrong," (and at the worst possible moment). Maybe I did have that outlook in my teen years (or perhaps earlier) that lingered into my adult life, but I fought hard to overcome it.

As a young teacher I heard a daily radio clip by Zig Ziglar called *See You at the Top* as I was getting ready for work each day. His early-morning radio spot gave a quick attitude message to help listeners change their thinking from negative to positive. His self-stated goal was to give the listener a "check up from the neck up" to eliminate "stinkin' thinkin'" and avoid "hardening of the attitudes". Like the renowned children's author Dr. Seuss, Zig Ziglar used a lot of little word plays to keep the listeners' attention. As a young 20-something adult, I bought his book called *See You at the Top* (Ziglar 1974). I remember so badly wanting to take it all in and make it who I really was on the inside in my thinking and attitudes. I read the book several times in the early years of my teaching career and independent adult life. It was a timely brick laid early on the road to a healthier outlook on life.

That being said, I want the reader to be clear in knowing that I did NOT find my healing through my own efforts toward positive thinking and a better attitude. I believe it was God who rescued me and is still rescuing me daily to this very day.

I love the Bible book of Joshua because it is so full of encouragements to go forth fearlessly and with courage. Joshua was one of the original scouts sent by Moses to check out the Promised Land for the Israelites after their miraculous release from the slavery of Pharaoh's Egypt. He and another scout, named Caleb, were the only two that came back with a good report and the motivation to enter the Promised Land. All of the other spies came back with fearful reports which led to cowardice and disobedience by Moses and the Israelite nation. Because of God's anger the whole party ended up wandering in the desert for another 40 years. After the eventual deaths of Moses and all of the men of military age, God decided it was now time to enter into His Promise, and He chose Joshua to lead the people across the Jordan River and into the land flowing with milk and honey.

Throughout this biblical book, Joshua is repeatedly encouraged to be strong and courageous and to lead the Israelite people into the land of their destiny. Joshua believes that God will go with him wherever he goes, and bring him success and prosperity. As Joshua obediently holds fast to his Lord, God does just as He said He would do.

Near the end of Joshua's life at the ripe age of 110, God reminds him, regarding his success, that, "You did not do it with your own sword and bow," (Joshua 24:12b). It was God who gave the Israelites land on which they did not toil, cities that they did not build, and food to eat from vineyards and olive groves that they did not plant (Joshua 24:13).

In the same way for me, I know that it was God who was my Rescuer. He provided me with healing from the wounds of my youth over the course of years. It was not just me changing my thinking and my attitudes. It was His grace and provision to give me exactly what I needed in specific times and places. The early brick laid by Zig Ziglar, with his quirky play on words, was motivation for me to see the importance of a positive attitude. Zig put into words what my dad so faithfully lived out daily. Those two men, with their words and their walk, showed me a better way to live. But, it was God who tuned my heart to that provision. He was there, in my mess, walking me through to freedom. I did not do it with my "own sword and bow", but by His strength and leading. All praise to Him who leads us forth in His strength and grants us His courage as we obediently rely on Him.

Chapter 48

As I reflect back on my very long road to healing,
I have wondered at times what is wrong with me that
I would let the pain from high school impact my life
for so long. I've come to the conclusion that **nothing
is wrong with me**. Every human being carries
baggage of some sort on this journey called life
UNLESS and UNTIL we purposely unload it
somewhere or onto someone. That's why professional
counselors and therapists will never lack for long,
hard work days!

I believe everyone has "stuff" in their life that they
would rather not admit to having to carry. It might be
the feeling of abandonment by a parent through
death or divorce, or being neglected by a workaholic
parent who was never there for you. Maybe a
grandparent or stepparent made you feel useless and
that you would never amount to anything. Maybe it
was a struggle with academic or learning issues that
impacted your confidence and ability to succeed in
life. Maybe the bar of success was set so high in your
family structure that no child could attain it and feel
worthy and acceptable. Maybe inappropriate sexual
contact by a family member, friend, or stranger left

you feeling dirty and unlovable. Maybe all you knew as a child was the hard work of a farming life and never had time to experience the growth of outside friendships. What I am saying is that everyone has experienced pain and disappointments in life. Along with that pain or disappointment can come serious impairment or destruction of one's self-esteem and self-worth. I believe that this is a common problem that many, or perhaps most, of us have been left to deal with in the best way that we can. It can leave us stumbling and fumbling along for decades causing us to miss out on God's very best for our lives.

Some people carry their baggage for years, dumping it off in chunks on the other human beings surrounding them, who are then obligated to carry or drag some of the weight, too. Those close to me may have been forced to carry a portion of my load without really understanding that load. That was not my intention, of course, but it likely happened to those walking their life's journey alongside of me.

People deal with their residual pain in many different ways. Sometimes it comes out viciously as in acts of domestic violence or an unexpected shooting that highlights the evening news, or in cruelty to innocent children or animals. Some people attempt to deny their pain and dull it with alcohol, drugs, illicit sex, or pornography. For some, pain becomes the driving force in a life spent trying to prove oneself valuable and worthy of love. Some may not even remember what specifically is causing their pain. They just know they feel damaged. Others, like me, turn their pain inward and hold it close to their hearts. Though you may not hear about it on the evening news, this, too, is highly destructive.

Stuffing your "stuff" doesn't work very well. It causes much unhappiness and a life of missed opportunities to find God's best. But, unless and until a person can find a healthy way to deal with past hurts, the pain **will** impact their life, in one way or in many ways, for as long as they let it. It took me a long time to figure out the best place to unload mine! Finally, day-by-day and step-by-step...my answer was God! Paraphrasing loosely, Psalm 129: 1–4, although I was greatly oppressed from my youth, the Righteous Lord has cut me free from the cords of the wicked!

Chapter 49

In 2015, singer Blanca Callahan released the album *Blanca*[1], and the song *Who I Am* (Callahan, Mosley, and Fieldes, 2015) spoke deeply to me about the daily choices I must make to live joyfully. The following simple lyrics hold a deep and valuable reminder for me and anyone else recovering from social rejection of any kind. The profound secret is in knowing where and to whom we must run! If you haven't heard this beautiful song, find a copy and listen with your heart. One source might be Blanca Callahan's online website http://www.officialblanca.com/

Who I Am from the album **Blanca**[1]

Another voice, another choice
To listen to words somebody said
Another day
I replay
One too many doubts inside my head

[1]Publishing: © 2015 Dayspring Music LLC/Group 1 Crew Music Publishing (BMI) (All rights Adm. by Dayspring Music, LLC)/ CentricSongs, 2 Hour Songs (SESAC) (Adm. by Music Services)/ Sony/ATV Music Publishing LLC, Upside Down Under (BMI) (All rights on behalf of itself and Upside Down Under adm. by Sony/ATV Music Publishing LLC) Produced by Seth Mosley
Writer(s): Blanca Callahan/Seth Mosley/Mia Fielde

Am I strong
Beautiful
Am I good enough
Do I belong
After all
That I've said and done
Is it real
When I feel
I don't measure up
Am I loved

CHORUS
I'm running to the One who knows me
Who made every part of me in His hands
I'm holding to the One who holds me
'Cause I know whose I am, I know who I am

I am sure I am Yours

Turning down
Tuning out
Every single word
That caused me pain
Unashamed
And unafraid
'Cause I believe You mean it when You say

I am strong
Beautiful
I am good enough
I belong
After all
'Cause of what You've done
This is real
What I feel
No one made it up
I am loved

CHORUS
I'm running to the One who knows me
Who made every part of me in His hands
I'm holding to the One who holds me
'Cause I know whose I am, I know who I am

I am sure I am Yours
I know who I am
I am sure I am Yours

Fearfully
Wonderfully
Perfectly
You have made me

I'm running to the One who knows me
I'm holding to the One who holds me

CHORUS
I'm running to the One who knows me
Who made every part of me in His hands
I'm holding to the One who holds me
'Cause I know whose I am, I know who I am

I am sure I am Yours
And I know who I am

Only God could bring the healing to my heart, mind, and emotions. No amount of self-talk, ignoring the hurt, or even Christian counseling could bring the healing that I desired. It was when I began running to God and centering myself in what He had to say to me, about me, that I found my peace. He made every part of me, even my lovely mouth. I am holding to Him as He holds to me. I know who I am because I know whose I am. What amazing grace that has been to ME!

Chapter 50

My middle name is JOY, and I had longed to lay hold of the destiny given me by my parents on the day that I was named. There were many years when the hope of lasting joy seemed unlikely. Now I know, for certain, that I was well-named and that JOY is my true and lasting destiny. My closest friends even call me Rosie Joy. I claim it, and know that God Himself has been on my side all along. If He had not been, I would have been a statistic, likely a victim of suicide. I was drowning in my pain and felt no hope. But He rescued me, not in the quick way that I had longed for, but in the slow healing process of a life spent following Him and looking for His answers.

God is a good, good Father, and I now believe that Jesus was praying for me as I entered my new high school for the first time. He was praying for me before that, through it, and in the many years since my graduation day. I was not aware of that, and I wouldn't have believed it at the time had someone told me. In hindsight and with the evidence of scripture, I firmly believe that Jesus was praying to His Father specifically for me. I did not know the turmoil and pain that was ahead for me. I couldn't have even guessed or imagined it, but He surely did. He knew what was coming even when I had no idea or inkling. He knew that there would be years of pain and insecurity as a result of the bullying leveled at me. He knew there would be many poor choices and decisions made because of my resulting low self-esteem and self-loathing. But He loved me and was on my side fighting for me in prayer. Just as Jesus prayed for His disciples and all believers in the gospels, I believe He prayed for me (John 17:20–23). He knew my story would eventually become His story. He knew my story could help others with similar painful stories to find His story in their lives, too.

In the days, weeks, months, and years of pain, I could not have believed that He was in it with me and for me. I could not have understood that He was interceding for me when everything seemed black and hopeless in my life. Without Jesus interceding for me, I would not be here to share my story. Instead, and granted it was a long, long path to trod, I have been made strong and have received my healing in the name of Jesus, much like the crippled beggar in the temple (Acts 3:1–16). My healing is evident to all who truly know me.

Praise be to Him, my Lord, who released me from the snare of self-hatred and brokenness. (s)atan, the enemy fowler, had me snared, in despair, and with no hope of rescue. But, God broke the snare, and I have escaped. My help came in the Name of the Lord, the maker of heaven and earth. I am out of the fowler's snare and free to FLY! (Paraphrased from Psalm 124: 2–8 NIV)

Reader, I pray that my story, with likely similarities to your own, will bring you cause for hope. No matter what secrets your story holds, God has the desire to set you free from the snares that satan has you tangled in. He longs to break the snare that will lead to your escape and let you fly! May your future hold joy and peace as you, too, lay hold of what God has to say about YOU!

Out of the Fowler's Snare
Psalm 129:1–4 (NIV)
A song of ascents.

They have greatly oppressed me
from my youth,
...they have greatly oppressed me
from my youth,
but they have not gained
the victory over me.
Plowmen have plowed my back
and made their furrows long.
But the LORD is righteous;
(H)e has cut me free
from the cords of the wicked.

Bible Scriptures used in *Out of the Fowler's Snare*:
Scriptures are from The Holy Bible, New International
Version [NIV] unless otherwise noted. See Appendix
for full passages.

Hebrews 12:1
Psalm 124:2–8
Ecclesiastes 3:1
Psalm 33:17
2 Samuel 22:5–7
John 8:44
John 10:10
Joel 2:25
James 1:19–20
Psalm 139
2 Corinthians 10:5
Romans 12:2
1 Peter 5:8
Matthew 6:14–15
Matthew 6:12
Mark 11:25
Luke 6:37
Ephesians 5:3
1 Corinthians 6:18
Proverbs 23:7a [New King James Version]
Philippians 4:8
Psalm 13:2
Isaiah 61:3
Joshua 24:12b
Joshua 24:13
John 17:20–23
Acts 3:1–16
Psalm 129:1–4

Appendix

Scriptures Referenced in Text
https://www.blueletterbible.org/
New International Version [NIV] unless otherwise
noted

In the Acknowledgments:
Hebrews 12:1
Therefore, since we are surrounded by such a great cloud of witnesses, let us throw off everything that hinders and the sin that so easily entangles. And let us run with perseverance the race marked out for us.

The Capture:
Ecclesiastes 3:1
There is a time for everything, and a season for every activity under the heavens.

Psalm 33:17
A horse is a vain hope for deliverance; despite all its great strength it cannot save.

2 Samuel 22:5–7
5 The waves of death swirled about me; the torrents of destruction overwhelmed me. 6 The cords of the grave coiled around me; the snares of death confronted me. 7 "In my distress I called to the LORD; I called out to my God. From his temple he heard my voice; my cry came to his ears.

John 8:44
You belong to your father, the devil, and you want to carry out your father's desires. He was a murderer from the beginning, not holding to the truth, for there is no truth in him. When he lies, he speaks his native language, for he is a liar and the father of lies.

John 10:10
The thief comes only to steal and kill and destroy; I have come that they may have life, and have it to the full.

The Rescue:
Joel 2:25
I will repay you for the years the locusts have eaten— the great locust and the young locust, the other locusts and the locust swarm— my great army that I sent among you.

James 1:19–20
19 My dear brothers, take note of this: Everyone should be quick to listen, slow to speak and slow to become angry, 20 for man's anger does not bring about the righteous life the God desires.

Psalm 139
1 You have searched me, LORD, and you know me. 2 You know when I sit and when I rise; you perceive my thoughts from afar. 3 You discern my going out and my lying down; you are familiar with all my ways.
4 Before a word is on my tongue you, LORD, know it completely. 5 You hem me in behind and before, and you lay your hand upon me. 6 Such knowledge is too wonderful for me, too lofty for me to attain. 7 Where can I go from your Spirit? Where can I flee from your presence? 8 If I go up to the heavens, you are there; if I make my bed in the depths, you are there. 9 If I rise on the wings of the dawn, if I settle on the far side of the sea, 10 even there your hand will guide me, your right hand will hold me fast. 11 If I say, "Surely the darkness will hide me and the light become night around me," 12 even the darkness will not be dark to you; the night will shine like the day, for darkness is as light to you. 13 For you created my inmost being; you knit me together in my mother's womb. 14 I praise you because I am fearfully and wonderfully

made; your works are wonderful, I know that full well. 15 My frame was not hidden from you when I was made in the secret place, when I was woven together in the depths of the earth. 16 Your eyes saw my unformed body; all the days ordained for me were written in your book before one of them came to be. 17 How precious to me are your thoughts, God! How vast is the sum of them! 18 Were I to count them, they would outnumber the grains of sand—when I awake, I am still with you. 19 If only you, God, would slay the wicked! Away from me, you who are bloodthirsty! 20 They speak of you with evil intent; your adversaries misuse your name. 21 Do I not hate those who hate you, LORD, and abhor those who are in rebellion against you? 22 I have nothing but hatred for them; I count them my enemies. 23 Search me, God, and know my heart; test me and know my anxious thoughts. 24 See if there is any offensive way in me, and lead me in the way everlasting.

2 Corinthians 10:5
We demolish arguments and every pretension that sets itself up against the knowledge of God, and we take captive every thought to make it obedient to Christ.

Romans 12:2
Do not conform to the pattern of this world, but be transformed by the renewing of your mind. Then you will be able to test and approve what God's will is— his good, pleasing and perfect will.

1 Peter 5:8
Be alert and of sober mind. Your enemy the devil prowls around like a roaring lion looking for someone to devour.

Matthew 6:14–15
14 For if you forgive other people when they sin against you, your heavenly Father will also forgive you. 15 But if you do not forgive others their sins, your Father will not forgive your sins.

Matthew 6:12
And forgive us our debts, as we also have forgiven our debtors.

Mark 11:25
And when you stand praying, if you hold anything against anyone, forgive them, so that your Father in heaven may forgive you your sins.

Luke 6:37
Do not judge, and you will not be judged. Do not condemn, and you will not be condemned. Forgive, and you will be forgiven.

Ephesians 5:3
But among you there must not be even a hint of sexual immorality, or of any kind of impurity, or of greed, because these are improper for God's holy people.

1 Corinthians 6:18
Flee from sexual immorality. All other sins a person commits are outside the body, but whoever sins sexually, sins against their own body.

Proverbs 23:7a [New King James Version]
For as he thinks in his heart, so is he.

Philippians 4:8
Finally, brothers and sisters, whatever is true, whatever is noble, whatever is right, whatever is pure, whatever is lovely, whatever is admirable—if

anything is excellent or praiseworthy—think about such things.

Psalm 13:2
How long must I wrestle with my thoughts and day after day have sorrow in my heart? How long will my enemy triumph over me?

Isaiah 61:3
...and provide for those who grieve in Zion— to bestow on them a crown of beauty instead of ashes, the oil of joy instead of mourning, and a garment of praise instead of a spirit of despair. They will be called oaks of righteousness, a planting of the LORD for the display of his splendor.

Joshua 24:12b
...You did not do it with your own sword and bow.

Joshua 24:13
So I gave you a land on which you did not toil and cities you did not build; and you live in them and eat from vineyards and olive groves that you did not plant.

John 17:20–23
20 "My prayer is not for them alone. I pray also for those who will believe in me through their message, 21 that all of them may be one, Father, just as you are in me and I am in you. May they also be in us so that the world may believe that you have sent me. 22 I have given them the glory that you gave me, that they may be one as we are one— 23 I in them and you in me—so that they may be brought to complete unity. Then the world will know that you sent me and have loved them even as you have loved me.

Acts 3:1–16

1 One day Peter and John were going up to the temple at the time of prayer—at three in the afternoon. 2 Now a man who was lame from birth was being carried to the temple gate called Beautiful, where he was put every day to beg from those going into the temple courts. 3 When he saw Peter and John about to enter, he asked them for money. 4 Peter looked straight at him, as did John. Then Peter said, "Look at us!" 5 So the man gave them his attention, expecting to get something from them. 6 Then Peter said, "Silver or gold I do not have, but what I do have I give you. In the name of Jesus Christ of Nazareth, walk." 7 Taking him by the right hand, he helped him up, and instantly the man's feet and ankles became strong. 8 He jumped to his feet and began to walk. Then he went with them into the temple courts, walking and jumping, and praising God. 9 When all the people saw him walking and praising God, 10 they recognized him as the same man who used to sit begging at the temple gate called Beautiful, and they were filled with wonder and amazement at what had happened to him. 11 While the man held on to Peter and John, all the people were astonished and came running to them in the place called Solomon's Colonnade. 12 When Peter saw this, he said to them: "Fellow Israelites, why does this surprise you? Why do you stare at us as if by our own power or godliness we had made this man walk? 13 The God of Abraham, Isaac and Jacob, the God of our fathers, has glorified his servant Jesus. You handed him over to be killed, and you disowned him before Pilate, though he had decided to let him go. 14 You disowned the Holy and Righteous One and asked that a murderer be released to you. 15 You killed the author of life, but God raised him from the dead. We are witnesses of this. 16 By faith in the name of Jesus, this man whom you see and know was made strong. It is Jesus' name and the faith that comes

through him that has completely healed him, as you can all see.

Psalm 124:2–8
2 if the LORD had not been on our side when people attacked us, 3 they would have swallowed us alive when their anger flared against us; 4 the flood would have engulfed us, the torrent would have swept over us, 5 the raging waters would have swept us away. 6 Praise be to the LORD, who has not let us be torn by their teeth. 7 We have escaped like a bird from the fowler's snare; the snare has been broken, and we have escaped. 8 Our help is in the name of the LORD, the Maker of heaven and earth.

Psalm 129:1–4
1 "They have greatly oppressed me from my youth," let Israel say; 2 "they have greatly oppressed me from my youth, but they have not gained the victory over me. 3 Plowmen have plowed my back and made their furrows long. 4 But the LORD is righteous; he has cut me free from the cords of the wicked."

Bibliography

Callahan, Blanca, Seth Mosley, and Mia Fieldes. *Who I Am*. Dayspring Music LLC, 2015. *https://www.air1.com/music/artists/blanca/songs/who-i-am-lyrics.aspx*

Farstad, Arthur, ed. *Holy Bible: The New King James Version: Containing the Old and New Testaments*. Nashville: Thomas Nelson, 1982.

Lerner, Alan Jay and Frederick Loewe. *Brigadoon*. New York: Broadway Ziegfeld Theatre, 1947.

Meyer, Joyce. *Battlefield of the Mind: 100 Insights That Will Change the Way You Think*. New York: Faith Works/Hachette Book Group, 2005.

Meyer, Joyce. *Battlefield of the Mind: Winning the Battle in Your Mind*. New York: Warner Books, Inc., 1995.

The Holy Bible, New International Version. Grand Rapids, Michigan: Zondervan Bible Publishers, 1978.

Wilkerson, David Ray, with John Sherrill and Elizabeth Sherrill. *The Cross and the Switchblade*. New York: Jove Books, 1962.

Wilkerson, Gary, with R.S.B. Sawyer. *David Wilkerson: The Cross, the Switchblade, and the Man Who Believed*. (Grand Rapids: Zondervan, 2014), p. 116.

Ziglar, Zig. *See You At The Top*. Gretna, Louisiana: Pelican Publishing Company, 1982.

Scriptures cited in the Appendix from online source
https://www.blueletterbible.org

Roseanne Joy Sanderfoot lives in northeast Wisconsin with her first husband and an old yellow dog. She lives to celebrate the destiny of her middle name. Her ultimate joy comes from God and His goodness, but friends, family, a classic muscle car, living close to nature, and a good cup of coffee in the cool of the day help fill her heart to overflowing. Roseanne's quest for joy has been long, but well worth the journey.

To contact the author: FreeRedBirdLLC@gmail.com

67850852R00157

Made in the USA
San Bernardino, CA
29 January 2018